BUYING TIME

BOOKS BY KIM BARTLETT

The Finest Kind
Gulf Star 45
Buying Time

GP85 00672

BUYING TIME

AN ESTABLISHED BUSINESS
FIGHTS FOR SURVIVAL

★   ★   ★

Kim Bartlett

LITTLE, BROWN AND COMPANY
Boston   Toronto

FIRST EDITION

Library of Congress Cataloging in Publication Data

Bartlett, Kim.
    Buying time.

    1. Corporations — United States — Case studies. 2. Corpora-
tions — United States — Finance — Case studies. I. Title.
HD2785.B24   1985   338.7'4'0973   84-21855
ISBN 0-316-08276-7

Designed by Patricia Girvin Dunbar

*Published simultaneously in Canada
by Little, Brown & Company (Canada) Limited*

PRINTED IN THE UNITED STATES OF AMERICA

DEDICATION

To Tatty and Q Bent — Whose enduring friendship is a most treasured gift.

Author's Note

Three years ago, the idea that developed into *Buying Time* seemed relatively straightforward, a slightly more sophisticated variation on the kind of book I had already written. These predecessors were "slice of life" books: I worked for relatively brief periods of time — for the first book as an offshore fisherman, for the second as a roustabout on an offshore oil rig, with the specific purpose of experiencing ways of life with the people living them. Then, I stepped back out of the way and wrote about these people while they, unperturbed by my disappearance, continued doing what they always had, as they always had.

What often evolved from these slices was a recognition of certain characters by the readers. "I used to work with a guy like that." This identification allowed readers to travel through ways of life that might otherwise be denied them, enlarging, in a sense, their brotherhood.

Buying Time also began as a "slice of life" book, the focus this time on the world of manufacturing and the people who do it. This was the initial premise: making things is what most of us do. We are surrounded by things, a large percentage of which are manufactured (as opposed to processed, grown, or constructed, for instance). Most of these we take for granted. They are there. *How* they got there is incidental; *who* got them there even more so — except to the people who took part in their manufacture. If you take a sewing machine, for example, and break it down into its many component parts, to the nuts and bolts, and ask: "Who made these?" you will suddenly realize that hundreds, even thousands, of people, of all types and persuasions, had a direct or indirect hand in the production of that one object.

This recognition, as the philosopher Bertrand Russell might have concluded, is trivially true. However, the trivial nature begins to wane when more "objects" are included and their respective parts multiplied. Now the hundreds and thousands become hundreds of thousands, or a work force and a way of life that have been the backbone of the country for decades.

To see faces beside bolts may require a poetic leap, but one that is not too farfetched. It is one that the reader is encouraged to make in order to embrace and enjoy *Buying Time*. Pennington Inc. is a pseudonym, but it is an existing company very much like any of those companies the reader passes by daily. And the characters in this book have their counterparts behind the brick, concrete block, or prefabricated buildings that contain that significant part of the work force.

When I embarked on this book I looked for an "average" company, and the Pennington Company came closest to that average. At the time the research took place the company was well-established, employed over two hundred people, had gross sales over $5 million, produced a recognizable product, and had a wide range of employees — men, women; skilled, unskilled; educated, semieducated; majorities, minorities.

How I located Pennington Inc., where it is located, and what it actually manufactures is both incidental and privileged information. I was given complete access to the company and its people, from Frank Pennington, the chairman of the board, to Pauly Ouellette, the "gofer," on condition that the company's identity be concealed and the privacy of its employees protected. Why I was granted such access is as much a mystery to me as it was to those who wondered why I was there, those who thought I shouldn't be there, those who probably lied or at least prevaricated a little, and those who probably said a little too much.

AUTHOR'S NOTE

For it was a trying time for Pennington Inc. The period I happened to take for my research accidentally coincided with the height of the recession of 1982. Companies large and small were daily smashing against the wall of extraordinary inflation and were crumbling regularly into Chapter 11 bankruptcy. Seventy-five-year-old, family-owned, family-run, third-generation Pennington Inc. was one of them. Like those of so many companies suddenly in crisis, its troubles lay largely with its reliance on doing things the way they had always been done. Its survival hung on its willingness to change, in some cases radically.

This unexpected jeopardy forced a change in my usual approach. My plan to step in and then out and to write a book stating that "this is the way it always is" was no longer adequate. No longer was I looking at people doing what they always had, expecting that they always would. Now there was the real possibility they might be doing it for the last time; that the next day, the next week, month, all of them could be on the street, jobless after all those years. Lives and ways of life were at risk. Vital decisions were being made. Basic values were in question. Unlike my past books, in which beginnings and endings were utterly arbitrary, this one had a beginning (which would have to be discovered), and an ending, which would come when Fate, not I, decided. All I could do was wait and watch, and do my best to record.

Buying Time is that record, the summary of which probably lies best in the following anecdote.

My first day at Pennington Inc. I had lunch with the recently hired vice-president/Manufacturing, Gerry Hanrahan. "Why us? We're just a little company out in the middle of nowhere," he said. Cautiously, I offered the "microcosm-macrocosm" theory. He listened politely but skeptically.

A little over two years later, the book wrapped up and in the mail, I lunched again with Hanrahan. We recalled what had taken place during the interim, both at Pennington Inc. and in

ix

the marketplace, noting how neatly the former reflected the patterns of the latter.

"It could have been luck," he suggested, half-heartedly.

Buying Time exists for two reasons: one, the story was there to be found; two, it was found. The first I had nothing to do about; the second I had a great deal less than my name on the jacket would suggest. The original idea belonged to my editor, Genevieve Young, who transmitted it over lunch to my agent, Carl Brandt. That was the easy part. It has been three years, countless letters, phone calls, typed pages, and probes and prods since that lunch, and I can testify that while I am the author, without Carl and Gene this book would not be.

It was also helpful having the goodwill and good faith of everyone at Pennington Inc. Without those good people there also could not have been a book, for they are the book. And there were others who helped set me straight in the beginning, who through their greater understanding of the project I was undertaking were able to line up my thinking. For certain reasons I can't name them, only thank them for their assistance.

And as ever, given the way I get through life, there are those who by being who they are make projects like *Buying Time* possible: Stan, John, Don, Dewey, Roland; Louise and David Marsh; the Parsons-Lovell, Lovell, Lewie, and Lois; Peter Davison, John Matson, and Dirk Wiersma; Mr. and Mrs. R. Rowland Stebbins; Mrs. Emeroy Burton-Bartlett and Donald L. Bartlett; et al. — thanks.

And last, but assuredly not least, there is my wife, Tudy, whose faith only infrequently flagged as she trudged off to work every day to keep me in board and bread while I held out promises. My sons, Dirk and Jake, would also like to be thanked, but are actually more thankful that this book is over and maybe, for a while, their father will be a little less grouchy.

Contents

1

Of Money, MAPICS, and Other Problems

★

The weekly executive meeting begins promptly at nine o'clock, every Tuesday morning. It is ten minutes before the first meeting of 1982, and while he waits until the last second, vice-president Barton W. Pennington sits in his office and drafts a memo to company president Donald C. Schmidt. There is a knock on his door. Receptionist Gladys Hale sticks her head in.

"Cup of coffee?" she asks.

"Please," he answers. Mechanically. For over thirty years Gladys has regularly fetched him his morning cup of coffee.

He puts his pen down and stares out the frosted window at the snow-covered yard, at the red brick and gray concrete block conglomeration of single-story buildings that makes up his family's company. The scene from his window has scarcely changed in all the years he's been with the company.

He starts a yawn and quickly stifles it with the back of his hand while he watches old Pauly Ouellette, the company "gofer," ease himself down the iced-up iron stairs at the side of the loading dock, and almost run to the company van. Off downtown to get the mail. Right on schedule.

This morning Bart had awakened early and had begun to dress to come in at seven-thirty as he had for so many years. Coming in early wasn't something he'd ever had to do, it wasn't a formal part of the job; it was just something he had always done. He would walk the back shop, say hello to the boys. If any of them might have a question, might need something, he would be there to talk to.

Bart knew them all. In some cases he had known the grand-fathers, and then the fathers and now the sons. He knew all the oblique relationships that bound the men together — and to Pennington Inc. He knew the passwords that got sons-in-law and cousins jobs and promotions — and, he would admit, kept some deadwood around. He was aware of the company's reputation, that once you had a job there, the company did its damnedest to keep you around, even if it meant the Penningtons themselves had to dip into their own pockets to do it. And they had, more than once. Loyalty was a two-way street.

"You gotta know the men, they gotta know you, gotta trust you," Bart liked to say, of late adding, warningly, "It's what pays off down the road when you are negotiating with them," suggesting a certain amount of expedience was mixed in with the altruism. He'd mentioned this to young Gerry Hanrahan, who had been brought in a month or so earlier to replace him as vice-president/Manufacturing. He'd mentioned it once, no more. Hanrahan was boss now. Bart was currently without portfolio.

Bart had stopped coming in early. In fact, he had stopped going into the back shop altogether. He had busied himself with the peripheral tasks that Don Schmidt farmed out to him and listened only as reports of problems filtered through the wall that separated the back shop from the front office. He had answered all questions asked of him, but he offered no unsolicited advice. He had put over thirty years of first-hand experience in the company on hold . . . until yesterday, when he'd had to go back there to speak to his good friend, plant supervisor Bud Darcy.

And he had seen for himself. There wasn't anything for the men to do. They ambled while loading the milling machines. They stopped and chatted while meandering from place to place. The forges were cast-iron cold. There was hardly any product on the floor. The only thing that was being made was work.

So today, he had gotten up early, like the old days. Beth had laughed and told him to get back in bed. He hadn't. He'd read the *Suffolk Times* at the kitchen table, suddenly said, the hell with it, and had come in and walked the floor again, checked the job sheets, and had returned to his office and written to Schmidt: "Owing to the lack of work coming in, I recommend that you seriously consider shutting down for a week in the near future."

Bart frowns as he folds the memo and puts it in an envelope. He has to lurch sideways to miss Gladys as he strides through the door to leave the memo on Schmidt's desk in the adjoining office. Gladys squeaks with surprise, spilling some of the hot coffee on her wrist.

"Sorry, sorry," he grunts. "Thank you. Thank you very much." And he walks away without the coffee. He pulls out a dead cigar from his coat pocket and sticks it in the right corner of his mouth.

Gladys shakes her head, turns around, and retreats to the nearby drinking fountain, where she pours the steaming coffee down the drain.

President Donald C. Schmidt is not in his office. He is already down the hall in the committee room arranging his notes.

Bart drops the memo on Schmidt's desk and starts to leave, hesitates, turns around, and neatly centers it between the pens and the black appointment book, which are regimentally ordered on either side of the blotter. The blotter's edges run parallel to the back of the swivel chair, which in turn is squared dead center to the desk.

He stops in the doorway and lights his cigar. Directly across the hall is a small office large enough for one desk and a chair on either side. No one has occupied that office full-time in over a year. Today there is a briefcase on the desk and an overcoat hung on the wall hook. And the overhead lights are on. Salesmen often use the office.

He inches up his cuff and looks at his watch, taps the small ash from the cigar, and heads left down the narrow, high-ceilinged hall toward the committee room. Bart is a slight man, whose body, though gradually sagging with age, cannot fairly be described as fat. Soft, yes. And stooping. He has the pallor of a man who has recently been sick and is still recovering. Bart is frequently ill, though never seriously.

As he enters the committee room and slides into his seat at the near end of the long table, a persistent, squeaky, "beep-beep-beep" sounds off from the other end. President Schmidt quickly pinches his wristwatch and looks up from the array of notes before him.

"I guess we can get started, gentlemen."

The committee room is long and narrow, roughly ten feet by fifteen feet, darkly paneled. Two bays of phosphorescent lights follow each other down the ceiling. Green chalkboards cover the top halves of the rear and right-side walls and a full-length mural depicting scenes of rural America covers the far wall.

The table is a rectangle with a glass top, the corners of which are chipped. The chairs are aluminum-framed straight backs, and not wholly uncomfortable provided you spend most of your time with your elbows on the table.

As president, Schmidt runs the meetings. He does this from his place in front of the mural. In the back corner to his right is an antiquated air conditioner. The first thing Schmidt always does upon entering the room is to flip the machine on. For the remainder of the session he will alternately turn it on and off, trying to maintain some balance between the need for fresh air in the windowless space and the aggravation of the machine's ancient wheeze.

Immediately to his right, in the first seat down the long side of the table, sits the chairman of the board, Franklin W. Pennington, Barton's first cousin and the longest-tenured employee in the company. Frank's presence is not mandatory, as he has supposedly retired from the day-to-day operations of his family's company. He continues to work full-time, however, and unless he is overseas on business or on vacation sailing, he attends. Frank is short, white-haired, impeccably dressed, the product of a well-absorbed private school–Ivy League education. He has stacks of papers before him. He culls, shuffles, and refiles them constantly throughout meetings, rarely looking up unless he speaks.

Frank always sits to Schmidt's right, and Barton always sits at the diagonally opposite corner, from which he can face both Schmidt and Frank. Whenever Schmidt looks up, he has to meet Bart's eyes — or he must consciously and obviously avert his by looking at any of the rest of the executives on either side of the table. Since Schmidt relieved Bart as vice-president of Manufacturing, Bart's eyes have seldom left him.

Harold Pennington, Frank's younger brother, generally tries to sit next to Bart. Bart is one year older than Harold, and both have worked at Pennington Inc. precisely the same number of seconds, starting immediately upon graduation from their respective Ivy League colleges. Harold is tall and thin and slightly taciturn. He either smokes or chews a briar pipe constantly, and is inclined to let Bart speak for him. Harold is vice-president of Administration as well as general manager of the company's Southern Division.

The rest of the seating is random, and often hangs solely on whim and promptness.

Tad Wilton really doesn't care where he sits. Tad would prefer to be at a draftsman's table. He shouldn't be vice-president of Engineering because VPs don't draw and create and spend lots of time thinking. They hire, then supervise, people who do those things. But Tad doesn't like supervising. He abhors paperwork. He detests office politics. He is disgusted by the picayune. If that is the way you are, then it certainly doesn't make any difference where you sit when the sitting is done where you don't want to be anyway. But Tad is a Pennington Inc. man and he appears obediently every Tuesday morning, politely answers all questions posed to him, doodles on the margins of the minutes of the previous meeting, and hushedly hums to himself.

Since the controller, Roy Fitzgerald, is frequently the last through the door, he is obliged to take whatever seat is available. As early occupancy is weighted away from president Schmidt, Fitzgerald more often than not finds himself next to or across from chairman Frank.

Like Frank and Schmidt, Fitzgerald carries with him a number of manila folders, which lie untouched until he is pressed for an exact figure to buttress a fiscal statement he has laid before the committee. Unlike most of the men around the table, Fitzgerald has spent most of his thirty-plus working years outside the aegis of Pennington Inc., and he frequently expresses views that run contrary to the others' perceptions. For his efforts he has been typed as a woe-sayer and is not taken as seriously as he thinks he should be. On the other hand, Fitzgerald is fifty-four years old and knows that his immediate future is tied to the company's. If he should find himself out on the sidewalk, he might be a long time finding another job. Thus he is willing to moderate his warnings. Fitzgerald is of medium height, heavyset, wears gray pin-striped suits, and slicks his thinning gray-black hair straight back over his crown.

Doug Searles, vice-president/Sales, tries not to sit at the table at all. If he can, he likes to be to the rear of Bart, a little to the side, and tilted back against the short blackboard. This way he can talk directly at president Schmidt — and, more important, chairman Frank — and past the rest of his fellow executives.

At forty-two, six-two and trim, Searles is considered the "bright young man" of the company. Three years ago, Schmidt's headhunters found Searles on the fast track of a large multinational corporation. The discovery was thought a coup for Pennington Inc. While he is nominally the head of Sales, Searles's professed expertise is in Marketing, which, he is quick to point

6

out, is the horse before Sales' cart. By extension, he argues, he who has a sense of the market's pulse, who can make accurate predictions and projections, is going to be the one who will make (or break, but this is not a factor) the company. Ergo, since this facility is his strength, among equals he is more equal, a position he attempts to symbolize by sitting back and expounding while the others sit forward — in silence. Unhappily, the three years Searles has been with the company have all been losing years, and his market forecasts have been off by as much as ten percent, which translates into over a million dollars a year in error.

Outwardly, Searles's confidence does not seem diminished. Until the recent arrival of Gerry Hanrahan, he had been able to point at Manufacturing as the drag on the performance of his men ("My men sell the product, but those guys can't produce it on time!"), but recently Manufacturing has been shuffling its feet waiting for work — and inventory has not been much diminished. The pressure on Searles is building. That it is affecting him is evinced by an increased tenor in his voice. Some call it whining.

As the "new boy," thirty-nine-year-old Gerrold X. Hanrahan of Manufacturing has been maintaining a low profile at the meetings. His position is awkward. He has replaced Bart, who over the past thirty years has developed a "good guy" reputation along with a long list of thank yous from the men under him. There is at least one generation of men in the back shop who have been raised by Bart. And in the front office as well, the rule of thumb is: "If you need something done, ask Bart. He takes care of his people." Now enters Hanrahan, almost twenty years his junior, a virtual unknown, another hotshot from the headhunters, a guy whose experience has been in the electronics field, whose education was vocational, not ivied like the three Penningtons' — and who is making twenty thousand dollars a year more than Bart has ever earned from his own company.

So Hanrahan sits wherever there is a place for him. He keeps

7

his mouth shut, opens it only when asked a direct question —
or when he feels he has not quite understood a point — and
otherwise smiles and remains attentive.

And finally there is the venerable Willis Farnsworth, vice-
president/Research and Design. Farnsworth is a big man with
a full head of white hair, a checkered sport coat, a too short, too
wide, yellow-on-black silk tie, and large, shaggy-browed eyes,
which gaze musingly upward at the tiled ceiling.

Farnsworth is the company's Pollyanna to Fitzgerald's Cassandra. If Fitzgerald's cup is always half empty, Farnsworth's is
always half full. He is a Santa Claus whose bag is constantly
filled with good news. Farnsworth's unfailing good cheer is
often a little too much for his colleagues, who treat him like the
company mascot.

And today, to Schmidt's left, is H. Edwin Blatchford. He sits
with his hands folded before him on the table, a chubby,
cheery, innocuous, grandfatherly man whose wide, innocent
eyes gently roam the faces of those gathered at the table.

H. Edwin Blatchford is a business consultant, a "company
doctor," whose specialty is restructuring faltering companies on
their way toward bankruptcy. He is the day's first order of business, and as Schmidt himself has only just been informed who
Blatchford is and why he is there, he turns the introduction
over to Frank, who brought him.

Frank clears his throat and neatens the stack of papers, then
looks up, first at Blatchford, then down the table at his brother
and first cousin. For reasons of his own, he had neglected to tell
them about the First City Bank's peremptory suggestion that
Blatchford be brought on board immediately if Pennington Inc.
hoped to have any chance of renegotiating its outstanding six-
million-dollar loan this coming March.

"Gentlemen, I'd like to introduce you to Edwin Blatchford,"
he says. "Edwin is going to be with us for a while. For how
long, I don't think any of us can say at this juncture. I've asked
him here to give us some advice as to how we are to handle the

next few months. He will be asking all of you questions, and you are to feel free to answer them as fully and candidly as possible."

H. Edwin nods to Frank and smiles benignly at everyone else.

"I'm looking forward to working with you," he says, and smiles again. Everyone nods and smiles back. This is the first executive meeting since the New Year's Eve layoff of over thirty men in the back shop and ten people in the front office. The reason for the layoffs was the unavoidable recognition that the company will have lost at least one million dollars by the end of the fiscal year. Orders have dropped dramatically since early October, and the new year looms as a greater disaster than the previous one. Layoffs and bad times are not new to Pennington Inc., but never in its seventy-seven years has the company had to go outside for help.

The wheezing of the old air conditioner is magnified by the silence that follows Blatchford's introduction. Schmidt reaches back and turns it off.

". . . Could run this company on the back of an envelope."

Schmidt has taken this opportunity to open the meeting with a lecture and he has adopted the tone of a scold. Running a company on the backs of envelopes is his favorite description of the ease with which things could be accomplished *if everyone did what he was supposed to.* Everyone has not, and that is why, he implies, the company is experiencing its current problems.

While Schmidt speaks, everyone else fiddles with papers, pencils, cuffs. No one looks at him. They have heard all or parts of this lecture before. It made no appreciable impact on them before and doesn't appear to have improved with reiteration.

". . . but, as Dr. Deming says, 'Eighty percent of all problems is system. If it is not there and not in place, you've got troubles regardless of what else you try to do.'

9

"So we've got to line out our priorities. We've got to map out where we go from here."

Schmidt holds up two sheets of legal paper — his priority list. All four sides are covered with orderly single-spaced, handwritten priorities.

"And number one, we've got to get the MAPICS system on-line and that means we've got to know what we are doing and we've got to communicate that to the people under us.

"I want you all to remember what we have learned these last few weeks working with Polaski: *measurements*. We've got to be able to get a hold on what is happening, and to do that we have to establish the measuring mechanisms. I've asked you all before to make an effort in this area, and, frankly, I've been very disappointed. To date I've seen no progress, no willingness. I'm aware you all have a great deal to do, and I know that each of you realizes this is a difficult time. But it is a time we must be pulling together. Natalie has packets of graph paper and I want you to take as much as you need and report back to me later this week on progress."

The assembled nod obediently, like reluctant schoolboys.

Six months earlier, Schmidt had attended a convention, and one of the speakers was a Dr. W. Edwards Deming, an economist whom the Japanese embraced during their rebuilding program after World War II. Deming is given a large amount of credit for the current efficiency of Japanese industry. His theory is predicated on the establishment of systems of accountability in which everyone knows what he or she does, what his or her relationship to the greater whole is, and why maximum effort is essential. Once you have all the parts working together willingly, production becomes simple. The key lies nestled in the measurement — of everything. It is the only way to detail inefficiency objectively.

Schmidt thought the concept was tailor-made for a place like Pennington Inc., which was operated as much by tradition and rule of thumb as by goals and orderly planning. Dr. Deming was not available to Pennington Inc., but a certain Polaski, who represented Dr. Deming in the area, was. So, for a fee that has now exceeded ten thousand dollars, the company has been exposed to systems and measurements through biweekly meetings between the executives and Polaski.

The whole matter has been considered pretty much of a boondoggle, a waste of both time and money, an insult and an intrusion. Bart was placed in charge of coordinating the affair, and, having very little else to do, he gamely appealed to the good corporate nature of his colleagues, so that attendance was better than might have been expected and assignments, though late, were eventually completed and presented. And the upshot has been that no one has learned anything, efficiency has shown no marked improvement, the yearly salary of one of the recently released secretaries has ended up in Polaski's pocket, and the men sitting around the table are quietly outraged as they realize that with all that has happened, Schmidt is still whipping that dead horse.

Behind Schmidt's back, Dr. Deming's systems are referred to as "another of Schmidt's Messiahs," one of his countless sure bets to lead the company out of the doldrums. Both Schmidt and Frank Pennington are notorious for their Messiahs. Every so often, they dovetail, like Schmidt's MAPICS with Frank's company computer.

MAPICS is a management system designed by IBM for its System 34, which the company bought a year ago and which has been idling in the basement waiting to be programmed. The 34 was bought to replace the Xerox copier, which cost the company three thousand dollars a month rental — plus another six thousand monthly in operating salaries — and was found to be too slow, too cumbersome, and plainly outmoded. And the Xerox itself had replaced the original IBM, which was too small from the outset, but, as a couple of disgruntled employees noted: "It satisfied Frank's need to be able to go to cocktail parties and say, 'Sure, we've got one!' "

In effect, the company has been operating in spite of its computer of the moment, but a year ago, Schmidt became convinced that if the company was going to continue updating models and paying the salaries of what had become an entire data processing department, it ought to incorporate the machine into the active management of the company. So, for fifty dollars an hour, a consultant was brought in to help Data Processing adapt MAPICS to the perceived needs of the company.

Like the systems and measurements, MAPICS has met with covert resistance. Charged with overseeing security in the system, Harold Pennington studiously took the two massive MAPICS instruction books home with him nightly, and later confessed to falling asleep over them.

Doug Searles says he understands the system, but argues that it is a rich man's toy and that the company cannot afford the luxury. Consequently, he resists MAPICS on general principles.

Gerry Hanrahan says he, too, understands MAPICS and, in fact, he has begun flooding his staff with reams of printouts while demanding more and more data from the beleaguered Data Processing staff.

Bart and Frank Pennington have assumed their right to have all they need to know presented to them in comprehensible form by those paid to draw it out of MAPICS. They don't care how it is done.

Controller Roy Fitzgerald says he is still waiting for the system to be made useful to him. Until that happens, he says, he'll continue contracting out the payrolls and having his people do their work the way they always have — by hand, with calculators.

And Schmidt cheerleads for MAPICS, rallying the boys, his normal monotone rising to counter the recurring wheeze of the air conditioner, and the boys are nodding "Yes, sir," while watching an imaginary clock on the wall.

"How are they taking the layoff in the back shop?" Schmidt suddenly asks Hanrahan, as though he has only just recalled why the buzzards are gathering on adjoining roof peaks.

"The people are pretty well resigned," Hanrahan answers. "They've known something was coming."

"I've got plans to let another thirty-eight go, and there are two retiring in the next couple of months," Hanrahan adds. "I'd say by the end of January a lot of things will probably settle down. It's a little bumpy right now, though."

"Thermo Electric just reduced its work force by twenty-five percent," Frank throws in, peering over his bifocals at H. Edwin Blatchford.

"They're talking layoffs at Honeywell," Schmidt says, as if trying to help Frank convince Blatchford that things at Pennington Inc. are not as bad as the bank has let on. Blatchford smiles and shakes his head sympathetically. H. Edwin is an old gunfighter. This isn't the first town he's been called in to clean up.

"Roy, what do the end-of-year figures look like?" Schmidt asks the controller.

"We sold one million, three hundred ninety-five in December," Fitzgerald reads from the top page of the top folder. "That's twelve million three forty-five for the year, with two million one thirty-six in accounts receivable." That's all he was asked for; that's all he's going to give. He passes a copy across the table to Blatchford.

"What's that mean in P and L, Roy?" Schmidt continues, as if he did not know.

"It can range," Fitzgerald enunciates carefully, staring at Blatchford. "A low could be in the three hundred thousand range; a high could reach seven hundred thousand; I'm guessing we'll lose around five hundred thousand."

There is silence around the table.

"The danger is, I project we'll need fifteen million in sales for 1982 to break even, and right now the minimum looks to be in the thirteen million range, so the loss is projected at a million three-oh-five," he adds.

"What's the story with Exten-Sor, Tad?" Schmidt interrupts, addressing the VP for Engineering. "Any progress to report?"

Exten-Sor Inc., a small label-printing company from Camden, New Jersey, has purchased a middle-range Marston Mixer from the company, and, according to Exten-Sor's engineers, the machine does not perform as promised. The Marston Mixer is Frank Patterson's most cherished Messiah. A machine whose time seems always on the verge of arriving, it continues to be plagued by problems that fifteen years of research have yet to iron out.

"We may be getting somewhere," Wilton answers. "We're running more tests today and should know where we are."

"We're being submarined on this thing, aren't we?" Bart bursts in.

"There is a speed problem," Tad answers amiably. "The machine will only go so fast. They want it to go faster."

"I hope you're keeping a data sheet so we don't get bagged," Bart states grumpily.

"I think the thing's a tempest in a teapot," Tad opines, with a slow grin. "Their engineers read the specs wrong. We're doing what we can. If it doesn't work out, it doesn't work out."

"That's a one-hundred-thousand-dollar machine. It had better work out."

Tad smiles at Bart. Bart does not smile back. Tad is having fun trying to make a machine do something it was not exactly designed for. He is being an engineer again. Bart knows that. He also knows that Tad could have assigned the job to one of his men, thereby freeing himself up for more office management. Tad knows that this is the third time Sales has tried to sell this machine and the third time the thing has come back because it failed to do what Sales had promised. He will personally save Sales' behind if he can, but he doesn't want to be scapegoated. He also knows that Bart is frustrated at not having anything valuable to do and comes to meetings with a quiver of arrows to shoot wherever he can.

Searles is palpably silent throughout the exchange. Schmidt is fidgeting.

"Harold, how're we doing with MAPICS?" Schmidt asks, separating Bart from Tad.

"Arnie Jax was in all last week, but I haven't heard anything from him so far this week. Sean Kerouac tells me the guy's building sound systems for his kid's rock band or something," Harold answers, tugging at his collar.

"Put a chain around his leg. Do what you have to," Schmidt says. "We gotta keep moving on this thing. Bart?"

Bart happens to have a few things to talk about. He has them listed on a piece of paper lying in front of him. He nudges the sheet out toward the center of the table so that he can check it, frown at Schmidt, have his say, and not have to move his head.

"We've got a security problem and it's getting bad," he states ominously. "There's too many people running around with keys and there's no one supervising what's going on. There's certain people should have keys and that's all should have them. I don't see any reason why half the people I find in here after office hours have to be here anyway. They should be able to get done what they have to get done during the regular day. I don't think we should be payin' 'em overtime, if we are, and if we aren't, they shouldn't be in here anyway."

"What sort of stuff's being taken?" Frank asks.

"Little stuff mostly, nothing big, but it adds up," Bart answers.

"You'd better call a spade a spade and talk with the individual supervisors," Schmidt suggests. "There shouldn't be any overtime being worked now anyway. I put a memo out to that effect two months ago."

"And some of the doors aren't being locked when people leave," Bart continues. "Last Saturday, I walked right in, the front door was wide open — and there wasn't anybody in *any* of the offices."

"Anybody in here last Saturday?" Schmidt asks. A general shaking of heads. "Anybody know of anybody in here last Saturday?" More shaking. "It could have been Pete cleaning up, taking some barrels out," he offers.

"I think we should get all the keys back and only those that really need one should have one," Bart grumbles, "but that will never happen."

"See what you can do, Bart," Schmidt says. "Doug?"

"We've got some good quotes out, but nothing is certain," Searles says, shuffling through his folders, then squinting up over his bifocals. "My boys say they're knocking on a lot of doors, but people aren't opening them any too wide. People are apparently going to stay with what they've got for awhile and see what turns up in the spring. It's bad out there, but, as I say, we've got a few good quotes and if they come through, January will be all right."

"Anything new with the Japanese?" Schmidt asks.

"I was talking with them Friday, and they are supposed to be back to me before the week's out. I get the feeling they are ready to run with us, if we can put together the right numbers. You get the same feeling, Frank?"

"I do. Definitely," Frank Pennington intones, chewing on the ends of his glasses. Frank's bailiwick is the company's foreign trade, and of late he has been courting the Japanese. The subject at hand involves a method that the Japanese have developed for making a very resilient paper that can be made to resemble various woods and, when applied to a hard backing like plywood or particle board, could replace veneers. He believes the Marston Mixer should be able to apply adhesive to the paper. He and Searles are very excited by the prospect. They see it as a deus ex machina. Others see only another Messiah.

"What we're trying to do," Searles explains, catching Blatchford's eye, "is get them to put up all the front money and limit our liability. They are being resistant, but they want a foothold in the American market and I think they like what we are doing for them." Blatchford nods and smiles.

"They're hot right now. We don't want to lose them. Presently they're not talking to anybody else, but . . .," Frank adds. Again Blatchford nods agreeably.

"Anything more, Doug?" Schmidt asks. Searles shakes his head, then removes his glasses and places them, in their case, in the inside pocket of his deep brown suitcoat.

"And Willis Farnsworth?"

"Well!" Willis erupts, squaring himself away in his chair. "I have some wonderful news from Sweden. They have been running tests on the Flomac and much to their surprise it measured up exactly as we said it would. They couldn't be more pleased, and I can't help but think this is going to mean many more sales as the word gets around how really very good this machine is. So I think you will agree with me, *that* is very good news indeed."

"That's wonderful, Willis," Schmidt says in a way that suggests the commercial is over. His colleagues are neatening their respective piles of folders, notepaper, doodlings, pencils, pens, glasses, coffee cups.

"Ah, just a minute, if you would," Farnsworth requests, his ready store of enthusiasm bubbling like lava. "As you know, we were able to sell the British a Whirlwind, and last month I went over to Coventry to advise them how to install it. Naturally I took along my trusty Kodak, and I thought you might be interested in seeing it in place."

From his pile he draws out three plastic sheets of color photographs of the Whirlwind, spick-and-span, in the company's yellow and green colors, surrounded by happy English faces.

"They are *ecstatic!*" he observes. "They want another as soon as possible. It astounds me how well this machine is selling overseas. I suppose it is merely a matter of time before our American market gets on the bandwagon."

Buried among the "ecstatics" and the "astoundings" is a barb for Doug Searles, whose salesmen have yet to sell a Whirlwind on their own. All national sales to date have originated either through word of mouth or through Farnsworth's personal contacts.

The Whirlwind is a huge pulper capable of reducing various waste materials to mush. Willis invented the machine. For some reason, Searles refuses to get behind it. This annoys Farnsworth, who, ever forgiving, seeks constantly for new ways to win Searles over.

Willis beams as the sheets of pictures are passed from hand to hand around the table. As an engineer, Willis likes concrete proof. These pictures show a machine and happy customers, evidence that at least in that place at that time people were pleased with a Pennington Inc. product; ergo, everyone around the table should be happy.

"Anything more, Willis?" Schmidt asks as the photographs come full circle.

"That's all," Willis answers.

"Then that's it for us, gentlemen," Schmidt says, rising. "Remember, Natalie has that graph paper. I want to see good response by this time next week. I also expect to be talking to everyone in the front office soon. Natalie will post the time on the bulletin board."

Even while he is still speaking, Schmidt has drawn his folders together and up under his arm. As he finishes, he is in motion toward the door. There is almost no chatter as the rest of the men file out after him, some turning right, most left down the short hall. Frank Pennington is the last to leave. Blatchford is just in front of him.

Frank and Blatchford do not talk as they turn first right, then left up the short incline. They stop at the door leading to Frank's office. His and Schmidt's joint secretary, Natalie Spangler, is typing at her desk by the window.

"I have a couple of calls to make, then I'm at your disposal," Frank says. "Anything you need, ask Natalie."

"I will and thank you," Blatchford answers, and continues his way up the hall. As he passes Schmidt's office, he sees him earnestly reading Bart's memo. As he stops before his own temporary office, he glances to his right, through the window in Bart's closed door. Bart is standing by his desk, looking out the window, puffing hard on his cigar. He turns around, sees Blatchford watching him, nods, and sits down.

Blatchford nods back and retreats to his desk, opens up his briefcase and takes out his calculator.

2

From the Beginning

★

C hairman of the board Frank Pennington's office is square, high-ceilinged, and windowless. What light there is comes from two ceiling fixtures and the doorway to the outer office where Natalie Spangler, the executive secretary, works. Natalie has a window with the same yard view Bart and Schmidt have.

Three of Frank's walls are maple-paneled, the fourth being partially covered with a false pink-marble veneer. Civic awards hang on two walls, a built-in bookcase is stuck into the third. Most of the books concern the paper industry; some involve local history. There are some photographs of his daughters taken when they were teenagers, twenty years ago. By the fourth wall is a table stacked precariously high with books, papers, folders, some aged yellow. His broad mahogany desk in the middle of the room is similarly heaped.

On the far left-hand corner of the old desk lies the December issue of *Tech Now*. It is folded open to a story entitled "75 Rewarding Years of Creative Technology." The article is celebrative. It consists of photographs of A. M. Pennington, the founding father; his two sons, S. R. and C. W.; their three sons, Frank, Harold, and Bart, along with the current executive board. There are also catalog pictures of the Flomac, the Whirlwind, and the Marston Mixer, plus an ancient photograph of the original three-room office building, built in 1912, which still acts as the entrance to and nucleus of the front office. The photographs wrap around a purported interview with Frank

Pennington. Much of it appears to have been pulled verbatim from an in-house monograph printed twenty-seven years earlier in celebration of the fiftieth anniversary.

It is a genial article and succeeds in its fraternal intent of making Pennington Inc. out to be a company on the move, upward; a company graced with a solid foundation and sensible business imagination; a company that has overcome the "rags-to-riches-to-rags" hazard so often typical of old family-owned and -operated businesses. There is nothing in the text that foreshadows the arrival of H. Edwin Blatchford, who, ironically, will soon take over one of the original three rooms for his headquarters.

The article begins matter-of-factly: "The company, originally the Wolverine Knife Company, was founded by my grandfather, Arthur M. Pennington, who was convinced there was a great opportunity to supply pulp and paper mills with better equipment. . . ."

Space and a touch of censorship preclude *Tech Now* from relating the full history of Pennington Inc. The tale, however, is familiar.

In 1905, Arthur M. Pennington, a short, rather severe man in dubious health, father of five, a bookkeeper at a local factory, took all the money he could muster and started a small company dedicated to the production of more durable industrial knives. In the fiftieth-anniversary monograph, Arthur M. is described as "having a keen interest in business" as a young man. "Even though no philosopher, while still in his teens he did subscribe wholeheartedly to the profit system — that principle which is the foundation of free enterprise and the 'American way.' "

In truth, his subscription was somewhat retarded. In an age that saw the rise of the robber barons, men who sought control of entire markets, not just small pieces, Arthur M. was a modest entrepreneur. He was forty before he decided to attempt his own business; and he funded his start with the savings of his five children and two thousand dollars backed by his life insurance policy (which, it is carefully noted by his heirs, he always kept current despite very little income).

"I have this day drawn from the Suffolk Savings Bank and deposited in the Beddington National Bank," he wrote on November 30, 1904, "the following sums belonging to my children: Silas R. Pennington, $1013.79; Caleb W. Pennington, $252.20; Arthur M. Pennington, Jr., $238.60; Matthew D. Pennington, $226.14; Abigail Pennington, $192.78; total, $1923.51."

In other words, Arthur M. began Pennington Inc. with nearly four thousand dollars, half of which came from his life insurance policy, the other half from his children's savings — and significantly, over half of the latter had been accrued by S. R., Frank and Harold's father, who could not have been more than twenty years old at the time.

The new company was named the Wolverine Knife Company. A forty-by-sixty-foot shed, later known as "the old boiler shop," was erected on land by the railroad track just across the green from the family's small house. Arthur M. reportedly brought five men with him from his last job, hired a bookkeeper-stenographer named Bernard Hull, who worked out of the Pennington parlor, and, on June 15, 1905, Arthur got his first order. It was for three hundred and six pounds of bed- and rag-cutting knives which, at eighteen cents per pound, equaled fifty-five dollars and eight cents.

Two years later, the company took in $37,823.50, and three years later, doubled that. The payroll grew from seven to thirty-three, and soon the accretion that was to be the company's architectural style began. In 1912, the original office building was built. In 1913, a twelve-thousand-square-foot plant was added to the "old boiler shop" (which even today is still useful for storage).

By 1917, it was decided that still more space was needed, so the "old forge shop" plus a mirror duplicate to the 1913 plant were constructed, along with two yard sheds for storing lumber.

It is noteworthy, in light of the present, that while the company was growing physically in giant steps, the funds with which to finance the enterprise must have remained marginal, for Arthur M. is reported to have taken his trusty insurance policy to the bank more than once as collateral for loans to pay off creditors. In the same light, by 1917, the payroll had jumped to eighty-two in the back shop and six in the front office. In 1982, sixty-five years later, after layoffs and forced and voluntary resignations, the payroll totals seventy-two in the back shop and a downward-spiraling eighty in the front office.

By 1917, Arthur M. had brought his sons S. R. and C. W. through the ranks into upper management, and by 1920 had virtually turned the business over to them, S. R. becoming vice president and general manager while C. W. was assistant treasurer, secretary, and sales manager. By 1921, S. R. and C. W. had bought their father out, allowing him to devote the bulk of his attention to playing checkers, albeit on the international level, while the sons took the company through the Depression and into World War II before succumbing to poor health. In 1941, Frank graduated from college, and by the mid-forties had practically taken the company over. By the time Harold and Bart joined in 1950, both S. R. and C. W. were dead.

Since its inception the company has remained under the strict control of the Pennington family. In 1916, the company changed its corporate name from Wolverine Knife Company to Arthur M. Pennington & Sons, Inc.; in 1960, to simply Pennington Inc., the latter signifying the completed course from A. M.'s action on an idea, through S. R. and C. W.'s expansion and solidification of that idea, to the grandchildren's custodianship.

Arthur M. had begun the company not so much with a dream as with a solid hunch that there was a place in the market for a product he felt capable of producing. And he had been right. Wolverine knives were well made. In a small corner of the knife marketplace Wolverine quality came to be respected and counted upon. And while the product could never be categorized as sophisticated, still Arthur M., and more directly his eldest son, S. R., made use of some advanced metallurgical technology to improve the product. The "heat treat" tempering and forging process the company still employs represented a courageous investment fifty years ago.

With updated variations, the bed- and rag-cutting knives that made up the company's first order remained the foundation of the company that came under the leadership first of Frank and, later in the fifties, of Frank and his brother and cousin. The company's share of the knife market at that time was modest but certain, and probably sufficient to provide the family with a respectable living.

From the middle fifties on, however, with the tacit approval of the Pennington family, Frank sought to broaden the company's portfolio. In 1958, an entire research and development laboratory was built and staffed across the street. In 1960, a European division was established. Along the way a series of small, ancillary companies were bought. All but three were soon resold, two currently servicing Pennington equipment, while a third forges special parts for pulping machines.

With such expansion came the need to increase revenue radically. As the industrial knives appeared to have achieved their maximum market potential, Frank began to redirect thinking and investment toward the production of capital goods. The Flomac, Whirlwind, and Marston Mixer make up the company's most recent offerings. The bindings of past sales catalogs burst with information on predecessors that the company brought forth with equally high hopes, only to scrap unceremoniously.

Frank's efforts to increase Pennington Inc.'s access to the marketplace led necessarily to increases within the operations of the company itself. A wider variety of products required a greater number of bodies to carry the products forth. Not only did the back shop personnel increase, but so did the sales force, now required to ply more numerous markets. Soon Pennington Inc. was supporting a regional sales force across the country while housing both marketing and sales staffs in the plant. The Marston Mixer alone required the full-time sales and design efforts of two men and the part-time service of most of the Engineering department.

Flomac and Whirlwind demanded as much attention, but the company couldn't afford the manpower. Even as it was reaching out toward the more glamorous capital-goods market, it was making its profits — or stemming its losses — with knives. Knives made up eighty percent of business, and eighty percent of knife sales came in unsolicited, sold by repeat order or word-of-mouth, not by salesmen.

And then the recessions of the mid-seventies came and sales drooped. The company survived, as it had the recessions of the fifties. Knives remained strong enough. There were shutdowns. Some people were let go. There were some empty desks. For a while. Then the economy started to flow, and Pennington Inc. geared up again. And the empty desks were filled again, and all the shifts in the back shop were working again. The only change anyone could see was that it cost a lot more to keep doing business as usual. Which meant that more product had to be sold. Which meant that more men had to be hired to produce and push the product. . . .

And then the recession of 1980 blew in. But it was brief and no sooner had the company felt its effect than it was over, like a one-day flu. Unnoticed during the recuperation, the early stages of the recession of 1982 slipped up and blind-sided the company, and now sixty-four-year-old chairman of the board Franklin Pennington, the man everyone still regards as the boss. the man who, as *Tech Now* described him, "wasted little time in rapidly expanding his family company throughout the world," sits behind the old, cluttered desk he took over from his father so many years ago, and waits for Searles of Sales to bring him the latest figures the Japanese have quoted on the Marston Mixer deal.

And just down the hall H. Edwin Blatchford, a complete stranger, a mandated interloper, is commencing a course of investigation that could lead Pennington Inc. out of the white-collar company kept by the Marston Mixers and back to the blue-collar basics represented by the old Wolverine Knife Company.

Frank isn't worried. He's seen controller Fitzgerald's year-end figures and he's seen Fitzgerald's projections. Something obviously has to be done. Layoffs have always sufficed in the past when problems arose. The company is still around. It will always be around. What's going on is nothing more than a reflection of a temporary downturn the rest of the economy is experiencing. If the Japanese deal comes through, everything will work out. If it doesn't, then they'll have to find something else to try.

3
"A Sense of Urgency"

★

President Don Schmidt is going to give a pep talk to the front office on Friday afternoon. As it stands, he will give it twice, over in the Pennington Research Center, first to the executive body, then to the middle management and secretarial staffs.

He has been thinking about this address for a couple of weeks, jotting down notes, talking to himself while driving home, bouncing ideas and approaches off his wife during supper. He had been up for it until yesterday when he had gone to the dentist — his teeth were hurting, all of them — and the dentist had informed him that they all needed capping, every damned one of them. Now, Don Schmidt is the kind of person who has not only been blessed with perfect, cavity-resistant teeth, but also with the proper discipline to maintain them. So why were these poster-perfect teeth in need of capping? He was grinding them. Sheer nerves.

This was the first big hint he was in trouble, that something was wrong and it involved him. It also put even more pressure on the speech than he'd felt to date. It is now incumbent upon him to transport to his fellow employees that faith he assumes he feels in the company. Together they will keep the place afloat, hold it on course through whatever seas might slam against it — and in the end everything will be all right, and he will be able to give his damned teeth a break.

Don Schmidt is a man who believes in sharing faith. For instance, in 1977, his first full year as president, the company enjoyed four hundred and forty-seven thousand dollars in pre-tax profits. It also employed two hundred and fifty people, up from the prior two years. There were no ominous clouds anywhere, and every reason in the world to keep the faith he had unswervingly embraced and adhered to from his youth in Kansas City.

That year, in his first annual Christmas letter to the employees, he wrote: ". . . We have problems, but we have strengths. I am certain that the strength of your combined attitude and cooperation will overcome any obstacle that we encounter. . . . Let's not forget to thank the One who has given us the blessings of a free land, opportunity, family, friends, and work. Let's also remember those who are not as fortunate as we, when we ask God's blessings for our endeavors in 1978."

The next year, another unencumbered year of record profits — eight hundred and sixty thousand dollars, pre-tax — and increasing employment — two hundred and sixty-eight — Schmidt sent a magnanimous Christmas greeting: "This year our country enjoyed another year of tranquility and prosperity. Even though people conspire and wage war in other parts of the globe, the Almighty has seen fit to bless Americans with peace. It is fit and just that we remember and give thanks at this time of the year."

As he entered 1979, Schmidt obviously felt in control of his and the company's destiny — with, of course, the aid of the Almighty. The fact that before accepting the job as president of the company the extent of his experience in governance was as general manager of a branch of a medium-sized paper company was of no consequence. He was where he was because he had worked hard and honestly, he'd done what he'd been asked, what was expected of him, and he'd shown sufficient initiative. The way to even this relative top had not been greased for him, but he was here. A few more profitable years and he'd be ready to step higher. Hard work and plenty of faith in the Almighty. A no-fail combination.

And then, December, 1979: "This year, Christmas comes

during a period of trial for both the Country and the Company. We have read and seen enough about Iran and the other spots about the world where our flag is being abused. I have communicated to you several times recently some of the problems being faced by Pennington Inc.

"Just as the will of the nation is being strengthened and unified to meet its test, so too will that of our employees, I am certain."

For the first time in three years, Schmidt refrained from attributing the results of the previous year to the Almighty's wisdom. In fact, the Almighty was never mentioned. Enter instead an abstraction that over the centuries has succeeded nicely in times of trouble — patriotism. In his next paragraph Schmidt draws the equation, rounding it off with a new declaration of faith.

"Pennington Inc. is a fine company with a history of seventy-four years. We have our faults. We also have our plans developed for the future and the strength to attain those goals. As with our country, Pennington Inc.'s strengths reside in its people, many of whom are second and third generation. We will be successful with the strength of such employees."

What had happened in 1979 was simply a one-hundred-and-eighty-degree turnabout from 1978. For, as the number of employees rose to two hundred and eighty, the second highest since the halcyon days of the late sixties, and gross sales rose nearly three million dollars to over nineteen million dollars, the company still managed to lose five hundred and sixty-four thousand dollars. Record sales, record losses. Although Schmidt did not hear it, the clock had started to tick. Back-to-back recessions were gathering way as he was wishing everybody a Merry 1979 Christmas and a Happy 1980 Year.

Schmidt's last Christmas letter was dated December 22, 1980. It began this way: "Last year when I wrote my Christmas message, I said it was a period of trial for both the country and the company. One year later, it is still a period of trial.

"Our people are still being held hostage. The Russians have

crossed the Afghanistan border and are poised on the borders of the freedom-loving Poles. War is raging between Iran and Iraq in the explosive atmosphere of Mid-East oil.

"At home the highest prime rate ever is threatening to push the nation again into recession, just as we had thought we had passed the crisis. Above all, the cancer of inflation spreads unchecked.

"Still, this is a time for hope and confidence. Whatever our political persuasion, the nation will soon have a new leader. It is hoped that campaign rhetoric can be turned to reality. It will take time and combined effort. Unfortunately, there is no quick fix.

"Pennington Inc. has performed bravely. Even though the recession bit deeply into our sales, we were able to cut costs and carry on the business. Frankly, I think our organization is stronger and performing better.

"Pennington Inc. enters 1981 with hope. It will be a difficult year, to be sure. Yet we do have some products whose time seems to have come. We do have new systems coming on stream. But most of all, we have you, our loyal people."

Schmidt's 1981 Christmas message consisted of the laying off of over forty people as Pennington Inc. faced its third straight year of near million-dollar losses. From a 1979 employee high of two hundred and eighty, the company was reduced to two hundred and thirty-six, the lowest since the recession of 1976, and within the first three months of 1982, that figure will drop to one hundred and sixty-six point-five, the lowest in over twenty years.

As Schmidt sits in his office, orating into his tape recorder, straining for the right combination of tones — tones that will project leadership with compassion, urgency without fear, confidence without complacency, but, most of all, a sense of pride coupled with unyielding faith in the company — he is aware that he is grinding his teeth again.

For Schmidt is in an untenable situation. As president of the company, he is where the buck stops. If the company is in trouble, he has to take responsibility even if, privately, he does not think he ought to, at least not as much as people are hinting he should.

Six years ago, when he signed on as the first non-Pennington ever to be president of the company, he had honestly felt the controls were firmly in his hands. He had lucked into an opportunity of a lifetime, the chance to take an old dog and, with skills honed from his marriage of a ten-year-old M.B.A. with nearly twenty-five years in management, to teach it new tricks. He had laughed when, at a conference down in Jacksonville, Florida, a fellow industry president had come up to him and almost chortled: "So you're Frank Pennington's head nigger." He remembered patiently explaining away that misunderstanding.

Just how Schmidt got the job is unclear. He claims that he heard the job was available, applied along with a number of other candidates, and was selected by a vote of the seven-member board of directors. Broadly speaking, Schmidt is accurate, with a couple of modifications. He had heard about the job from Frank, who at that time was president of Consolidated Industries, a large state lobbying organization of which Schmidt was also a member. Whether Frank offered Schmidt the job on his own or whether he told the Pennington board he had an excellent candidate and let the board have the illusion it was making a decision is the speculative part. All parties seem to remember there being other candidates, but none recalls ever meeting them. The fact is, Schmidt entered the company as Frank's handpicked successor and there wasn't much either Harold or Bart, both equal shareholders with Frank, could do about it.

If either Harold or Bart had wanted the job, it would have been his for the saying so. Neither did. There were reasons, ostensibly health, which was also allegedly why Frank was

31

stepping down. For while the founder, Arthur M., had lived into his seventies, his two sons had died relatively young. Frank had always suffered from asthma; Harold had nearly died of cancer; and Bart was perpetually on the verge of one sickness or another. The constant threat of a premature death, the natural frailty of their bodies, their increasing age, and the realization that not one of them had a child the least bit interested in joining the company had convinced them all that the time had come to begin infusing the top echelon with new blood.

The nice, perfectly intelligent, well-mannered, pleasantly dispositioned, adequately experienced, morally impeccable, unflamboyant, "company man" Schmidt seemed ideally tailored for the nice, perfectly intelligent, well-mannered company owner Penningtons.

His arrival caused barely a hitch in the company's business-as-usual momentum. "I want somebody to tell me what to do," Bart told Schmidt the first time they met. Fair enough, Schmidt thought.

And even now, as he reruns the past six years through his recollection trying to find some absolution, Schmidt has to admit that both Harold and Bart cooperated one hundred percent "in their minds." But, as he had reiterated to his wife, Penny Sue, the other night on the way home: "You can't treat owner-employees the way you would simple employees. You want to make changes, they find a way to obstruct, even if they don't want to. They won't move things along. They don't want to make decisions, but they aren't sure they want you to, no matter what they say. And when you're operating a company, you can't wait around for years. They don't understand that. They've never any of them known any other way of doing business than the way they've always done it. Which they believe is the right way. You try to talk managerial concept with them, it's like you're talking Arabic; and there's no one there who speaks Arabic."

Ironically, the boldest move Schmidt has made to date was

the removal of Bart as vice-president of Manufacturing and the hiring of Gerry Hanrahan to replace him. And the luckiest! Hanrahan is *brilliant*. It won't be long before that back shop will be unrecognizable. Unfortunately, the removal of the chairman of the board is not within the president's prerogative. If it were . . .

Right now, as he enunciates into the tape recorder, he has risen above that mean line of thinking. He is a man with a mission, a man with a message, a frustrated but resolute man. A man trying desperately to convince himself of what he has labeled "a sense of urgency."

A tall, tired, out-of-shape man, his sleeves rolled up over pallid arms, the skin on his face slack and grayish, eyes pouched, brown hair graying and receding, sideburns cut off slightly above the earlobe level. He sets the hand microphone down on the glass top of his desk, tilts back in his swivel chair, his left leg crossed over his right knee, and stares out through the high multiple-paned windows at the yard.

It is still very cold out. The wind is whipping, but the snow on the ground is old and crusty and only partly covers a pile of rusted steel bars lying alongside the far wall of the long, dingy brick Building Number 1 to his right. A forklift skids around the far corner by the wood shop across the yard to Building 2, which parallels Washington Street, its operator heavily bundled and hunched over, a scarf flapping in the face-on wind rifling in from around the building's corner. A T&P Transport truck is backing up to the loading dock. A couple of men run flatfooted between the buildings. In the foreground he can see the white of Frank's new Peugeot station wagon parked just below the window. Beside it is Bart's Buick station wagon and Harold's Oldsmobile sedan, all company-owned. His own Toyota Celica isn't there. Penny Sue had taken it for the day.

He shakes his head, as if trying to get his senses back, and spins around in his chair to face forward at his desk. With purpose he snatches up the mike, leans forward, almost glaring at the opposite wall, on which hangs a framed blueprint of the first pulper Pennington Inc. ever produced.

"Eighty-five percent of the problem is *system*," he states, stopping just short of waving his free hand in the direction of the wall. "With the right system we could run this place on the back of an envelope. And *that* is why I have brought in MAP-ICS. And that is why, with your cooperation, we are going to make MAPICS work."

He stops and, reaching to his left, reverses the tape. He punches the recorder — STOP . . . PLAY — then hangs his head meditatively, his eyes fixing on the family picture stuck under the glass on his desk — Penny Sue sitting, and himself and the three boys towering over her. A nice, healthy, honest family, a source of encouragement. There is a plaque on the inside wall made up of a big gold arrow and an inscription: "Don Schmidt — the Straight Arrow Award." That was from the boys last Christmas.

". . . is *system*." Schmidt nods. ". . . have brought in MAPICS and that (*"that,"* he says aloud to the picture) is why, with your (*"your,"* he modulates) cooperation we are going to make MAPICS work."

He snaps off the recorder and smiles. He is pleased and ready to wrap the speech up. He presses PLAY and RECORD and picks up the mike.

"I am very optimistic. We have the products, plant, the people to turn this thing around, but it is going to depend on you. *I* am going to need *you* to carry us through. This is no Chinese fire drill. It is serious business, there is a very real sense of urgency needed, and I don't want to have to stand up here six months from now and tell you, 'That's all she wrote, folks.'"

He knows he doesn't have to listen to that last part. If he can recreate that same intensity, he can't miss. Schmidt stands up, straightens some folders on his desk, then strides to the door, where his suit coat and overcoat are hanging. He puts them on, flicks off the lights, and walks slowly down the corridor to the outside door at the end of the Engineering Department. He is off to lunch with Penny Sue. Three out of five lunches he has with his wife, now that she has gone to work at Arlen's Corp. just across the tracks. Before he'd usually eaten alone. Of late he'd begun lunching with Hanrahan, when Hanrahan stopped for lunch, which was rarely. In six years he has never had a lunch with a Pennington that didn't have specifically to do with business. Once, four years ago, he was invited to Harold's house, he and one hundred other people.

4

Willis and His Whirlwind

★

Most people who know agree that the Pennington Research Center (PRC), and everything that goes on in it, is vestigial. The main reason it has not been excised is the underlying rationale that established it in the first place back in 1958: "It shows people we're no fly-by-night operation." Any company that maintains its own research lab has tomorrow in its plans. The fact that the lab has a staff of two, and that one is a gofer, does not diminish the initial impression that there is probably something going on there that might be important.

What is going on, of course, is the Willis Farnsworth Show, as smoothly orchestrated a piece of barking as one could hope to find this side of the last traveling medicine show. Or so it could be construed by someone who didn't know Willis's inherent wealth of enthusiasm and pride in his product. He is the only one in the company who actually sells what he alone conceives, creates, and, in many ways, constructs. And he sincerely believes that all his products will do exactly what he says they will, if you'll just let him show you.

At the moment, Willis is performing his Whirlwind Act for a wallpaper company located in northern New York State. Five employees, chemists for the most part, made the trek south late the night before, and Willis has had them in PRC since eight o'clock A.M. sharp.

But the Willis Farnsworth Show did not begin then. It got started a month earlier with a phone call to Willis from out of the blue. Listen to Willis — with a perfect stranger:

"Terrific . . . I'm delighted. . . . Exactly . . . oh, it's great down here . . . really? ah, yes, it's a product for our times, I'm amazed . . . it lives in two different worlds. . . . Ahhhh! . . . Ha, ha . . . Do you have any descriptive material? . . . Good. Wonderful . . . People come here fully expecting it to fail . . . and they give me an order before they leave. . . . No problem, no problem at all . . . it would be my pleasure. . . ."

Now that same stranger is standing beside Willis, and together they are watching a pipe spew forth a grayish liquid into a large tank. The stranger has on a white lab coat over a plaid shirt. He is short, overweight, wears glasses that steam up as he peers into the tank, and seems both obstinate and unsettled. Willis is dressed in a light blue polyester three-piece suit. His coat is off and his white shirtsleeves are rolled up to his elbows. His tie is black-on-white, with odd dashes of maroon through it, and is snugged to his neck.

"I think we're getting closer," he yells through the overpowering roar in the large, high-ceilinged room to the stranger, whose name is Art. Art waves commandingly to another square man who is standing, a white bucket in hand, on a platform by the spewing pipe. He swings his bucket under the mouth of the pipe. The gray matter splashes and spits over his arm, onto his face. He quickly fills the bucket and disappears through a door behind Willis and Art.

Willis raises his hand over his head, waves it around a few times in a set of tight circles, then makes a cutting motion with his fingers outstretched. In the far corner of the building a young man jumps to his feet, goes over to the wall, and tightens down some valves. Silence sweeps into the room. Everyone disappears into the adjoining lab.

What is being demonstrated is an enormous blender whose function is not dissimilar to that of the standard kitchen variety. In fact, Willis has often experimented with an old Waring Blender before performing his act publicly with what the company calls the Whirlwind. What the Whirlwind does is take waste products such as shoe boards, or denim, or gasket material, things that have traditionally been carted to landfills and buried (at great expense and waste to the companies) and pulverizes them, reducing them to a substance capable of being reconstituted into the original product. This is accomplished by creating a terrific race of water around a large vat. The race picks up the scrap material, driving it through finely calibrated, whirling grinders, around and around until the material is a solution.

And that is the rub. Because the material has already been hardened off and is now being returned to a soluble state, little hard lumps of undissolved material often remain. The reclaimed solution will only make up thirty percent of the end product, but it must be consistent in texture with the other seventy percent. A correct balance of grinding time, water temperature, and chemical breakdown additives must be concocted to treat the recalcitrant particles.

And here is the game that Willis and Art are playing. The faster, more efficient, and less expensive the process, the happier everybody will be. Willis knows that the Whirlwind will handle this wallpaper "broke." He wants to experiment to see how few chemicals he will need to break the material down. Art is frustrated because he wants to see success instantly. At this juncture he doesn't believe Farnsworth. He is feeling as if he is the butt of a humorless joke.

But Willis has another string he is pulling. He knows he can do what's necessary, but he wants Art to have that singular feeling that he, not Willis, was the one who, through experience and insight, has come up with the proper balance. It is a shuffle-step Willis has danced countless times before.

"They all come down here like this, thinking that because it's their product we're working on, they know more about its properties than you do. It doesn't pay to tell 'em otherwise. All you'd do is offend them and make them harder to convince. . . . Now, what's happening is, I'm letting this guy experiment for himself, letting him discover what the Whirlwind can do. I'll guarantee you, before the day is out, he's going to be a believer. But right now is where I've got to be careful. All these other guys with him are along for the ride, but they have to seem important. If they get the idea that — what's his name? — that he's unhappy, they'll join him. It's tricky."

There is a third party involved in the show who has perhaps a more immediate interest in the success or failure of the demonstration than either Willis or Art. He is Mack Spring, one of the company salesmen. Whirlwind sells for around one hundred thousand dollars. Mack gets a percentage of that. Willis collects no royalties as the inventor; Art gets only credit or blame if his company buys one, but Mack can take the sale to the bank.

And there is nothing Mack would like more right now than a good sale. There have been a lot of miles between them, a lot of hours spent in reception rooms in the middle of some awful wastelands, a lot of motel rooms and lousy meals and Scotch and TV movies . . . but definitely a lot of miles, which get longer and more tedious the older you get.

And there are a lot of miles on Mack. The lines at the corners of his eyes resemble the tracks of a flock of hens. He stands there in the lab just behind everyone, but close enough to appear interested in what's going on. The effort involved in just appearing interested is almost palpable. It would be so easy to sit back in one of the chairs and close his eyes, just for a minute, and drift off to the Big Rock Candy Mountain, where commissions hang like oak leaves, and all you have to do to get one is wake up in the morning and take a long, relaxing stroll and reach up every so often and pick one off.

Mack is dressed in a three-piece dark blue pinstripe suit that could well have come from a bargain basement. His dark brown oxfords are polished but scarred. His hair is gray, cut short and combed, but is somehow scraggly. His face is pink and he wears bifocals. He is of average height, and heavy. Mack has worked for Pennington Inc. for fourteen years, the first ten handling the Midwest, the past four the Middle Atlantic states. He has a year and a half until retirement. Mack has been a salesman all his life, having never once been brought in from the cold.

Mack is still amazed that Art and his crew are here at all. It was simply by accident that he dropped into their home offices. He never had before, and he's still not certain what prompted him this time except a what-the-hell, you-can't-lose-anything incentive coupled with the real need to sell something.

And he'd nearly walked out without a sale when at the last minute Art mentioned all the scrap his company throws away, and how he'd certainly love to save the money he spends getting rid of it and buying its equivalent in new stock. And how it was getting that the landfills were about to refuse the stuff, which meant hauling it even farther. So Mack laid the Whirlwind on him, and here everybody is.

Of course, if it weren't for Willis, there would be no hope for a sale, because Mack knows nothing about the Whirlwind. It had never occurred to him to tell Art: "I'll bet you have a scrap problem. About everybody does . . . and we have a machine guaranteed to solve it." This unaggressive, unimaginative approach is what is driving Willis crazy about Doug Searles and the entire Sales and Marketing force. He has compiled a list of the types of materials the Whirlwind can handle. The possibilities are wide and varied. He has brought the list to Searles and has suggested it be passed on to all the salesmen.

"Do you realize how many companies are implied on that list?" Willis tries to explain. "If only half of them bought Whirlwinds . . . and they can pay for them in six months from the savings . . . and . . ." And that is where the matter remained. There were other, more pressing issues . . . like the deal with the Japanese. Real glory jobs which could bring in big bucks, if . . . instead of a few hundred thousand from a few Whirlwinds . . .

And what was it that Schmidt said to Willis just last week? "Willis, you've got a lot of contacts in the industry. Why don't you get on the phone and make a few calls, drum up some interest?" This from the president to the only person in the company paid to be creative; this from a president with a sixty-thousand-dollar-a-year vice-president of Sales and a department of ten salesmen sitting strategically around the country. Willis walked away from that one shaking his head, momentarily stunned and finding himself almost thinking like Cassandra Fitzgerald.

Willis looks at his watch.

"Art," he says, "this batch we'll heat the water up a little more, and let's say we run it for twenty-five minutes."

"I'd recommend adding the cutting solution to it," Art grumbles.

"Excellent! Excellent! Fine!" Willis responds as though a light bulb has just been turned on for him. "But first, it's almost twelve noon now and it will take an hour to clean the vat and refill it. What do you gentlemen say about some lunch?"

There is an assortment of agreeable grunts.

"Good. Good. There is a nice little place just around the corner. Mack, lead on."

Mack reacts much like a lineman who suddenly finds the ball in his hands. All morning he has remained discreetly in the background, making appropriate noises, but being as innocuous as possible. His sentences have run the length of "That looks a little better, wouldn't you say?" or "That's more like it." Positive-sounding buzzes and no more. And now the show has been turned over to him, the bearer of the credit card.

The nice little place around the corner is called Renko's, the place to go if you like very ordinary executive lunches in the near total absence of sunlight. It is the kind of place middle-management persons take one another when there is no deal on the line.

Mack finds a table long enough to seat everyone and takes

the end seat, leaving Willis and the others to their own. Mack orders a glass of rosé, Willis a V-8 juice, two of the wallpaper group have beers, two more say "Thank you. Nothing." And one wants orange juice. It seems that he overslept breakfast at the Sheraton Motel they are all staying at, and all he'd eaten since last supper was a doughnut.

The visitors gabble away like old turkeys about the Sheraton. It is evident that none of them get out of their northern New York State towns very often, and then it is usually to go duck hunting or snowmobiling up-country.

Mack has a steak, Willis scallops, the others hamburgs with fries and chef's salad. The oversleeper has a western omelette with a side order of sausage. One of them starts a story about rabbit hunting. It's a "one that got away" story, of which the teller is the butt, and everyone laughs. Which happens to remind Willis of a "Did you hear the one about?" story. It is a typical Farnsworth tale and Mack, who has heard a number of them in his day, retreats deeper into his silence, his eyes dully facing the table, picking up nothing in particular. He chews deliberately as Farnsworth, almost giggling in anticipation of the punch line, rattles on about the three rabbits — Pft, Pft-Pft, and Pft-Pft-Pft — and how while eating Farmer MacDonald's cabbage Pft gets sick and dies . . . and not too much later, forgetting the past, the remaining two rabbits return to the patch, eat more cabbage, and of course, Pft-Pft gets very sick . . .

". . . so Pft-Pft-Pft calls in the doctor, who looks at Pft-Pft and announces, 'Pft-Pft is very sick. Pft-Pft may die.'

" 'But,' says Pft-Pft-Pft, 'Pft-Pft can't die.'

" 'Why can't Pft-Pft die?' asks the doctor.

" 'Because we've already got one Pft in the grave,' " Willis concludes and breaks into booming laughter.

There is a brief hesitation before smiles break out and a ripple of laughter lightens the lunch. Which is all Willis intended, for he has determined that this group is somewhat ill at ease, confused, feeling out of place, and Willis believes that work is work, but lunch shouldn't have to be work, too.

Or at least not the whole lunch. Still, a little bit of salesmanship might not hurt. So, he launches into how tickled some tobacco companies have been with the Whirlwind and how the English mint just bought two and they are "ecstatic."

Willis has to be careful naming names, because a lot of the companies he has sold to view the machine as a foot up on the competition. Pennington Inc. has had to agree in writing that its salesmen would never disclose the purchase to the competition. This can be troublesome, for the best advertising is word-of-mouth recommendation and living up to the Joneses. Flyers, brochures get thrown away or skimmed at best, but when you can say: "R. J. Reynolds has one and loves it," you've added some weighty credibility. Willis knows, for instance, that within fifty miles of the wallpaper company there is a Whirlwind "and they're working out details for a second." But he has been sworn to secrecy. It's frustrating.

Art is getting itchy. He looks at his watch. They have to be back at their plant in the morning. It is a six-hour drive, more if the predicted snow comes. And he is well aware that for at least three of the guys this trip is a junket. It keeps them happy, makes them imagine they are vital, but it is costing the company money, which is tight, so he'd like to get on with the business at hand.

"Well, I'd imagine we've got ourselves another batch about cooked up," Willis says, looking at his watch and taking a final swab across his lips with his napkin. "Thank you, Mack. That was just what the doctor ordered." Willis is careful to give Mack all the credit for the meal, which the Pennington Inc. credit card Mack is putting back in his wallet had paid for. Mack nods. Throughout the meal Mack has uttered no more than fifteen words over and above those directed to the waitress.

The afternoon is almost a replica of the morning, batches of wall-covering "broke" chewed up by the Whirlwind under varying conditions, then spewed out to be tested for solids and adhering strength. As tests improve, so does Art's nature, and more and more Willis defers to Art's suggestions, until by the afternoon's end Willis is nodding while Art is talking, with enthusiasm, about the Whirlwind.

Finally it is agreed that given all the configurations they have tried during the course of the day, they are probably on the verge of coming full circle. Willis suggests that they all adjourn to the conference room above and "shake down what we've all learned."

Unlike the conference room in the main building where the executives hold their weekly meetings, the PRC version bears a fair resemblance to one's idea of a corporate conference room. It is nicely paneled — dark — with indirect as well as direct lighting. A long glass-topped table, comfortable chairs, bookshelves, a green chalkboard, a sideboard with a new coffeepot, cups, sugar, Cremora, and stirrer, and pictures on the wall, large, glossy color photographs of Pennington Inc. equipment in action. In this conference room you can tell what the company does, which is one of the reasons that very important meetings involving banks and boards of trustees are held here and not back across the street.

Willis is standing at the chalkboard, in one hand a piece of chalk, in the other a pointer. He is finishing up a chemical explanation of what has been happening all day. In the space of four minutes he has covered the blackboard with graphs and formulas and diagrams and arrows connecting all manner of things. Laying the pointer down in the chalk tray, he says: "There's a very short story which I think you will agree sums this whole day up perfectly." There is a perceptible slumping in respective chairs. Willis grins.

"A scientist and an engineer are put together at one side of a room, a lovely young lady is standing against the opposite wall. They are told they may move toward her but only half the distance each time. You are all well aware of the principle in effect here. Finally the scientist turns to the engineer and says sadly, 'So close yet so far away.'

"The engineer looks at him, then at the girl.

44

" 'Close enough,' he says, and walks away with her."

There is a roar of genuine laughter.

"Thank you," Willis says. "I've enjoyed the day," and he reaches across the table and shakes Art's hand. The other four stand up and alternately shake Willis's. Mack stands by the door, waiting to open it..

An hour later Art and his crew head back to their north-country homes. Willis never heard from them again.

5
"... On His Knees"

★

Don Schmidt gave his "sense of urgency" speech to the entire front office at three o'clock Friday afternoon, a full two weeks after the first major layoffs were announced, the same day a week's shutdown was posted. It took about half an hour to get everyone across the street to the PRC, to get their collective attention, and to enunciate properly the salient points while also underlining them in red on a large pad folded over a nearby tripod.

Afterward everybody dispersed to their respective offices to wrap up the week's work before leaving for the weekend. Many of them had looked forward to Schmidt's talk. They had begun to admit openly that maybe something was more than just wrong, that it might be more than a worsening economic crisis; that it might just have to do with the company's idea of business-as-usual. What they expected from Schmidt was a plan of attack, something specific they could actively start implementing on Monday. They were ready.

For they were becoming scared. Many of them had been there their entire working lives — twenty, twenty-five, thirty years. Their fidelity extended past debt, obligation, and love for Pennington Inc. to a quivering fear of the "other world" they had never known. And their fear was buoyed by a disbelief that they in the front office, they so close to the seat of decisions, might be expendable. When they talked of "teams" in the front office, they were not referring to the Pennington Golf Team but rather to "us here, the family."

So, when bodies started falling in numbers, the empty desks

46

took on ominous overtones. For it wasn't just the lower levels that were being tapped out. In October, the treasurer "resigned". There were personal reasons, everybody said. The treasurer was easy to explain away.

In November, the personnel director "resigned." It was rumored that he and Schmidt had had a personality conflict, but it soon became obvious that with a decrease in personnel to direct, and with a decrease in orders and thus income, the position was rapidly becoming redundant.

Then to everyone's amazement, in December, Bart Pennington was replaced by Gerry Hanrahan, whom no one had ever heard of. It was one thing to shuffle and change bodies whose sole connection with the company was professional, but to start touching the family, to realize that even the Penningtons were vulnerable! To see someone like Bart, who had established his rightful territory in the family business early and had held on to it for so many years, to see him give it up (willingly or not, it was hard to say) to an outsider and accept the amorphous title of "vice-president and assistant to the president" . . . Bart Pennington, the most popular of them all, cashiered . . . If that could happen, nothing was sacred, no one was safe.

They all had a right to be scared, and they had a right to expect that their president would show them a road, any road, to safety. That was why he was making $60,000 and they were making a third of that at best.

And instead he had given them the same old pap, the old "things are tough out there, but I know you can do it, guys and gals. Let's get in there; keep fighting for God, Country, and Pennington Inc." routine into which were snuck the buzz words — *systematize, prioritize,* and the ever-present "back of an envelope." They'd all heard it before, in the corridors, in the parking lot, even, for those whose timing was bad, in the men's room.

So they went back to work for the last hour of the week, back to the way things were, had always been, probably always would be.

Gladys Hale went back to her receptionist cubicle in time to flick a flashing red switch and snap out a particularly waspish "Pennington Inc. May I help you?"

Gladys Hale. Short, bulky, churlish, yet there, always there. Since 1950, a month after Bart and Harold graduated from college and came to spend the rest of their lives at Pennington Inc. with her. Cute little Gladys O'Leary. Fresh from high school, a darling of a thing, and as snappish then as she is today. For thousands of customers, hundreds of wives and children, husbands, that apparently "put-out-with-life" voice had been the sound of Pennington Inc., a cantankerous assurance of the continuity of things. Unknown is the number of potential customers who took their business elsewhere after catching Gladys in an off moment. None of them know the Gladys Hale who daily shares her lunch with the pigeons on the green while she chats happily with an old Park Department maintenance man she has befriended.

And Johnny Hardy, the assistant controller, went back to his desk in Finance and literally pushed papers around until he heard controller Roy Fitzgerald enter the adjacent office. At that point he stuck his oversize briar pipe between his teeth, laid a match across the bowl, sucked the flame down through the firmly tamped tobacco and the reservoir of slurp, let the smoke gush out around the stem, and then ambled into Fitzgerald's office, where he dropped lumpily into the red easy chair.

Johnny Hardy is forty-five years old, and has been with the company for twenty-two of those years. About five years ago he tried to leave. He sold his house, packed up the wife and kids, and moved to northwest Florida, where an old friend had said there was plenty of work, good money, and multiple chances to improve his "life-style." Six months later, Johnny raced back. The company embraced him, and now life is as always.

This is not to say that he has given up hope of improving his life. When he is not being an assistant controller, he is an Amway salesman. It takes very little to divert Johnny from his columned figures to a discourse on his Amway dreams, which he has bought in their entirety.

What Johnny wants to talk to his boss, Fitzgerald, about are some expense vouchers from a couple of men in Sales. These show a suspicious pattern of Saturday dinners for two at local restaurants. Fitzgerald guesses that one of the diners is his young, attractive, single-parent secretary. He has been trying to warn her away from this situation, but evidently she hasn't listened.

"I'll talk to Searles about this again," Fitzgerald says. "Kind of tells you what the guy thinks about the company's bottom-line problems, doesn't it?"

Johnny puffs and slurps at his pipe. "Just thought you might be interested," he allows. Johnny has worked under a number of bosses. He has survived by being only obliquely involved. A couple of words dropped here or there, especially around Natalie Spangler, the executive secretary, is all anyone needs to get things done.

Gene Scola, the production manager for Building 1, went back to his office and buried himself in blueprints and work orders the way someone might pull covers and comforters up to block out a frigid room. Gene's office is cluttered with books, magazines, manila folders, lunch bags, seed and tool catalogs, and pieces of clothing. Much of the mess hails back nearly two decades.

Gene is a tried-and-true, home-grown product of Pennington Inc. He is forty years old, mustachioed, and heavyset, with the mien of a cobbler or a cigar store owner. He has been with the company for eighteen years. The company has paid for his education. It has brought him slowly up the line, nurturing him constantly until today Gene exudes devotion from all pores. If there is anyone in the company whose head is farther down, whose butt is farther up, whose push is any greater, who can be steered in more directions with the complete confidence that he will do his utmost to accomplish whatever the task is, that person has yet to surface.

Gene's only weakness is that his nose is so close to the grindstone that all his eyes pick out is grit. Distinctions of the most flagrant shades frequently escape him. He is often shocked, surprised, and personally hurt by certain truths that are clear to everyone else, that seem to have been sprung on him by a capricious deity. For instance, right now he would gladly assassinate Don Schmidt. . . . for once again just being Don Schmidt, and not Moses.

Ida Bright sat down at her desk, reached over to a file cabinet, pulled out the middle drawer, and drew out a folder labeled "February." She laid it on her desk and opened it. She then rolled a clean sheet of white paper into her typewriter and commenced to write: "Arnold Noble — 23 years . . ."

Arnold Noble was followed by "Jack Barney — 23 years" and "Ed LoPinto — 22 years," and on through "Sean Kerouac — 3 years." The company "honor roll." It isn't due for a week, but there was something about Schmidt's talk that made Ida want to get it done. The "honor roll" is posted monthly in its own case on the wall across from the bulletin board and the door to the ladies' room. It simply lists those who were hired during that particular month and how long ago the hiring took place. It is a source of continuity for a lot of people.

Ida can practically compose the list from memory. She will be on the March list — 32 years; six months longer than both Bart and Harold. She is a tall, single, attractive, shy person who has been the personnel director's secretary almost from the outset of her career. From time to time she has had a direct boss; other times, like the present, she answers only to her own dictates.

For Ida, either way is fine. According to controller Fitzgerald, Ida is the quintessentially average Pennington Inc. employee. She arrives at five minutes to eight every morning, stops exactly at noon for lunch (which she eats with the other "girls" in the conference room), takes precisely twenty-nine minutes before returning to her seat, and leaves at four-oh-five. "She doesn't stop doing something all day and, when she's finished, she has accomplished almost nothing."

When she had typed "Sean Kerouac — 3 years," she cautiously drew the sheet out, set it in the folder, and returned the folder to the file drawer, pushing the heavy drawer in with her foot. Then she got up and went to the ladies' room down the hall.

Dan Hutton, director of Purchasing, didn't say a word to anyone as he wound his way through the halls to his office out by the "old boiler room." As he passed through the canteen, where some of the men from the back shop were grabbing a quick cup of coffee, he was stopped by shop steward Hod Grady of the packing room.

"What'd the guy say?" Hod demanded to know, plucking at the sleeve of Dan's perfectly tailored sport coat.

"Nothing. Fucking nothing," Dan answered, stepping out of Hod's reach, through the door, onto the breezeway, and left into the Purchasing office.

His assistant, Frankie Lombardo, and their half-time secretary, Arlene Hoague, materialized suddenly from behind a partial screen used to divide up some of the open space in the office. Dan gave both of them a resignedly disapproving glance and continued into his office. Arlene blushed and giggled and sat down at her typewriter. Frankie went into Dan's office.

"What did Schmidt tell us?" he asked, half curiously.

Dan was fiddling with the Rolodex on his desk, turning it around and around, staring at the white cards with names and numbers tumbling after each other like a Slinky.

"Jesus, you gotta feel sorry for the guy," Dan said, more to himself than Frankie. "When he began he was strong, forceful. You had the feeling that maybe *this* time he'd say something

. . . by the time he was done, he was on his knees . . . he was, like, begging us. . . ." Dan banged his fist on the desk.

"You know what I can't understand?" Dan continued, looking past Frankie. "Why now? Why not six months ago, a year ago? Why'd he have to wait until the bank stepped in and threw this old guy Blatchford on top of us? It kinda gives you the feeling these guys don't know what the hell they're doing."

This was not the first time Hutton had arrived at that conclusion. In fact, it was occurring to him so regularly he imagined he could set his watch by it. And he was beginning to put some pieces together, at least those that concerned him. Here he was, thirty years old, head of a purchasing department that had employed five when he'd begun two years ago and now consisted of two and a half, in a company with no forseeable future, run by well-intentioned men whose idea of business practice had either been handed down through the family, derived from books, or overheard. In other words, for someone with ambition and prospects, every day spent at Pennington Inc. was a step to the rear.

He waited until Frankie left his office, then he got up, shut the door, sat back down, and made a telephone call to Harding Construction Corp. in Wallington.

Sean Kerouac went down to the basement where the IBM System 34 computer was housed. He was half inclined to continue working on the program Hanrahan had asked for, but . . . it was so close to quitting time . . . and it was Friday . . . and he'd be in on Saturday anyway since there wasn't much else to do now that the wife and kids had moved away and since he lived just on the other side of the green. So, well, Sean decided that maybe he'd call it quits early and slip over to the Ward 8 Franco-American Club for a few pops and a little think about things.

So he did. No one saw him leave because he used the side entrance to the basement and cut through the yard gate and down along Washington Street, putting Building 2 between him and anyone who cared. Then he crossed the snow-crusted green by the old bandstand, and over to the Ward 8 Club.

Sean sat down at the end of the bar that stuck into the banquet room. He ordered a double Seven and Seven, hung his jacket over the back of the stool, pulled down his tie, and yelled at the bartender to turn up the fucking sound on the tube, what was on anyway. Sean is forty-two and has seen his share of hard times, some compliments of the Fates, some directly from his own production. He has been with the company for only three years, having started in the back shop as a gofer. Gene Scola had obtained the job for him, as a favor. Sean had been closing in on rock bottom. "I'm taking a chance. Don't screw up on me," Gene had said.

Sean hasn't screwed up. In six months he was out of the back shop and into the front office working directly under Scola in Production. At about that time the IBM System 34 was bought, and as no one in the company knew much about the machine, and that included Tommy Lee McRainey, head of Data Processing, Sean reckoned that with a little effort he could make himself indispensable as the only one around who could operate the thing. By the time Schmidt got around to hiring a consultant to help Data Processing out, Sean had his niche carved out. And while the answer to the question: What does Sean Kerouac do? is usually: "How the hell should I know? Something to do with the computer, I think," that is enough to have kept him around when employees with far more seniority have received their last paychecks.

All this makes Sean feel expansively true to Pennington Inc., especially after a couple of hours and more than a couple of Seven and Sevens. Which is why he has Lyle Driscoll by the arm. Lyle has worked in the wood shop for thirty-four years. He is one of those who have seen the company ride through its many ebbs and flows. He has a draft in one hand, a cue stick in the other, and has just yelled over his shoulder: "I'm coming as soon as this jerk-off lets go."

For the past five minutes Kerouac has been extolling the virtues of one Gerry Hanrahan, who, he swears, is "fucking brilliant" and who is going to "straighten this fucking company right the fuck up," provided — and here is his point — provided Schmidt and the Penningtons let him. Of course this brings to mind Schmidt's "sense of urgency" speech, which Kerouac has repeated almost verbatim, punctuating his points by squeezing Lyle's arm and enunciating: "This company's in real trouble, man. You guys in the back shop have got to do something. You got to get together and do some fucking thing except bust Hanrahan's balls when he asks you to do something."

"Kerouac, you're a raging asshole! What do you know about nothing? You wasn't brushing your own teeth when I first started in the back shop. The company's always going through bad times and they do all right. When you see Frank's not driving one of them Mercedes or Volvos or whatever the fuck he drives, you tell me and I'll toss in my paycheck to bail the place out. Otherwise, go screw yourself, you crazy frog bastard, and that fucking hard-assed mick that took Bart's job."

Lyle tries to yank his arm free of Kerouac's grip.

"You're not listening to me, man. This company's going down the tubes. We gotta help it. We gotta stick together, you and us, both sides of the wall, to save it, man. I'm telling you, things are bad."

"Up yours, Kerouac."

6

Defections, Departures, Dismissals

★

T he first defection is Tommy Lee McRainey. However, Tommy Lee has been so clever in his timing that no one reads it that way. In late December, he announced that he had been offered a new job closer to home, with more money and a company car . . . but, by golly, he'd give Pennington Inc. another month of his time because he didn't want anybody thinking Tommy Lee was a rat. That made Tommy Lee seem so good no one asked whether he had gone out looking.

It was also about that time that the cold fact of a near million-dollar loss for the year was settling in, and guys like Don Schmidt and the idle Bart were beginning to look around for available heads to lop off. And, as Tommy Lee was fond of saying, "Mrs. McRainey didn't raise no pretty baby, but she didn't raise no dummy neither." He could read as well as anyone, he was occupying one flagrantly superfluous position, and while his $30,000 a year wasn't out of line in the marketplace, it was, for Pennington Inc., "a pretty fair piece of change."

Tommy Lee is the head of the Data Processing department, which is located in the basement directly under the executive offices. He was hired by president Schmidt five years ago to program the old Xerox computer. There are those who said that the company wasted a lot of money on a machine — and a position — it didn't need, particularly as the machine couldn't possibly do half of what was wanted. Tommy Lee agreed with the former and succeeded in convincing Schmidt to purchase a more sophisticated machine that really *could* improve the company's means of doing business. This was the now notorious

IBM System 34. It also meant that everything that had been entered into the Xerox, plus the myriad of data the Xerox hadn't been able to incorporate, had to be programmed into the 34. This produced the happy result of too much work for Tommy Lee and his crew of three to accomplish. To speed programming along, he persuaded Schmidt to hire an old friend named Arnie Jax as a consultant at fifty dollars an hour. With the arrival of Jax there was even less than usual for Tommy Lee to do. Which was tolerable so long as the boat was making headway and no one was bothering to look too closely as to how all the parts were functioning. But, when gray started to form on the horizon and the seas became a little choppy, Mrs. Mc-Rainey's baby commenced looking around.

Now his spell at Pennington Inc. is about over. He has exactly an hour and ten minutes on the payroll, then he drives away for what should be the last time. He is feeling good, yet lonely — and surprisingly sober. He has just returned from a luncheon in his honor. Practically the whole front office had shown up. But in that far corner of his heart that he reserves for doubt, he wonders whether he might have been an excuse for a little relief from the increasingly joyless atmosphere that has settled into the front office.

It had been a pretty good party, and real fancy, the way ol' Tommy Lee likes things to be. About forty of the staff, including Don Schmidt and Harold Pennington had shown up, put down five dollars a head for chicken or lamb, cooked Lebanese, french fries, and peas. Drinks were cash, and about everybody had beer except for Tommy Lee and Sean Kerouac, especially Tommy Lee. Everyone wanted the honor of buying him a round of his favorite Jack Daniel's, until Tommy Lee had to stand up and make a public announcement that "thank ye, kindly" but he guessed he'd do just fine on what he had in front of him at the moment. Which kind of burned those who had been aiming to get Tommy Lee a little shitfaced before the meal was over.

Tommy Lee had been in good form, sitting as the guest of

honor at the center table, flanked by Harold Pennington and Don Schmidt. Bart Zola, his assistant, and Arnie Jax held down the corners. Long tables jutted off the ends so that everybody was seated in a U, which made yelling up at Tommy Lee and him yelling back pretty easy.

There was only one trouble with the affair: the fun lacked fun. The barbs that should have passed for banter seemed to have real points on them. And when Tommy Lee said how he guessed that with so many people turning up he probably had a friend out there somewhere, you wondered whether he really believed the odds.

For you have to understand that Tommy Lee was an anomaly at Pennington Inc. He was loud, he could be offensive; he dressed oddly, talked crazily, and had certain personal habits that could worry a strong stomach. Plus, he was a stranger twice removed; neither a native (a West Virginian of all things!) nor a Pennington Inc. retainer.

And there was a gnawing suspicion that he was full of shit most of the time, but that wasn't what bothered people. It was that he also didn't give a damn about Pennington Inc. And maybe if he'd not given a damn and just kept his mouth shut, he would have at least been appreciated as a character. But, to use his own expression, he kept telling everybody "where the bear crapped in the woods," that is, the truth as he saw it. And he was frequently on target. Which wasn't hard. Anybody who had been down the road a couple of times could have been, if they'd had a mind to. But no one did. There was too much invested.

They all clutched tightly to the safety of their numbers, to the abundant homogeneity, to the "family" of the front office. There were no Jews, no Arabs, no Puerto Ricans, only four Italians, a couple of Poles, one black (who was actually an African, a draftsman who stayed at his table), five Germans. With these exceptions the front office broke down more or less equally among the Anglo-Saxons, the Irish, and the French Canadians. If there was racism or exclusion, it was inadvertent. People came and stayed. When a job became available, there was always a friend or a friend of a friend ready to take it. Thus, the office makeup simply perpetuated itself year after year. It is easier to work with people you feel comfortable being around, people like yourself, people you've grown up with, in fact.

In a sense, Pennington Inc. was a blissful dead end. Half the people had started work there and had no inclination to leave. For others it was their second or third job, and once they'd arrived, they knew they had a safe harbor. For a few, particularly the sales force, Pennington Inc. was the last stop before coming to roost forever. The company was a place whose easy if sometimes disjointed ways they had become accustomed to. They were raising families, paying mortgages, buying motor homes and motorboats on loans predicated upon the solid name of Pennington Inc., and upon the certainty that it would always be there for them — and they there with it.

"So they've all got to be covering their asses," Tommy Lee would point out, loudly. "There ain't a one of 'em's going to take blame for something if they can switch it off onto someone else."

Which was a rough thing to say about a group of people you worked with, whom you presumably had to get to work with you. Yet he said it anyway, and in a way that kept people off balance and uneasy.

For you have to understand, Tommy Lee is right about one thing: Mrs. McRainey's baby ain't pretty. He stands five-nine, maximum, and weighs out at close to two hundred pounds. His brown hair is thinning, and he has a neatly trimmed moustache which cannot camouflage the tobacco-stained, chipped front teeth. His face is pouchy and there is a scar that runs horizontally across his left cheek.

But Tommy Lee is a careful and studied dresser. As you walk down the stairs from in front of the conference room to his office at the foot, the first part of Tommy Lee you see are his boots — genuine leather, polished to a fare-thee-well. These are crisscrossed on his desk or stretched out to the floor. The pants are carefully creased dress khakis, into which is tucked a pink shirt held in by a broad leather belt with a big brass buckle. A leather vest fits over the pink shirt, a paisley tie is pulled down from an open collar, a brass chain necklace is visible around a reddish neck. On a hook on the wall behind him hangs a dark brown blazer with brass buttons. Tommy Lee dresses to feel like *dynamite*.

Compared to the majority of the men in the front office, Tommy Lee is a peacock, an image he obviously cultivates — and neatly destroys when he picks up one of the two Styrofoam cups he has on his desk, plucks off the plastic lid, and expectorates a stream of brown chaw juice into it, replaces the lid, and sets the cup back next to its neighbor (which holds his Cremora-brown coffee). It is a habit that has twice the negative affect that bad breath has on serious conversation.

But with Tommy Lee, conversation is a one-way street, for, honest to the good Southern tradition he says he hails from, Tommy Lee is an inveterate storyteller. And while he attempts to pass off all he says as "the simple and damned truth," his stories are better enjoyed as prevarications, embellishments, or good, old-fashioned, harmless lies.

For example, here is his life story, paraphrased and decidedly abbreviated.

He was born forty-one years ago in a small mining town in the southwest section of Pennsylvania. But as a mere baby he was transported across the state lines to the coal district of West Virginia. At this juncture Tommy Lee was too young to be able to claim any extraordinary feats. These were in the offing, however.

When he was eight he began hustling pool at a hall owned by his uncle. He would take his newspaper route money and parlay it through eight-ball into grocery money for his poor mother. (It is not part of the story what happened to Father McRainey.) When he graduated from high school, he signed a professional baseball contract and was assigned immediately to a triple-A farm team. "But I got hit with a high, hard one and

59

was never able to throw again."

His alleged baseball career in shambles, he joined the navy and immediately signed up with the Seals, the navy commando unit, only to find himself in Vietnam as an "advisor." At this point commences a set of events reminiscent of the late Audie Murphy: "Eighty-nine confirmed kills" . . . delivering native babies in the midst of brush fires . . . escaping a POW camp and "carrying my buddy the last two hundred miles" . . . to finally ending up in a Veterans Administration hospital in a complete collapse, from which, he says, he has yet to completely recover.

As the tale unwinds he is prone to tears and, when he looks at the photographs of his two children on his desk, he apologizes and stops, choked, wiping his eyes with a worn white handkerchief, before stating that due to "something that happened long ago" he will not live to see those children grow up. Like the mystery of the missing father, he does not elaborate on the fatal "something."

And that is the Tommy Lee McRainey to whom forty-plus people have gathered and paid five dollars a head to pay tribute — or perhaps just to get out of the office. And for which they got to watch Bart Zola mumble a few incomprehensible words before handing over a gift certificate good at any Anderson-Little store. To which Tommy Lee said, "Thank you," then stood up and allowed as how just this very night before the present goings-on, he had felt the Muse stir, and together they had composed a little poem. Which he read. And you could hear the Lawrence Welk orchestra in the background. Gene Scola, Sean Kerouac, and Rick Carney tried to keep straight faces, not because of the schmaltz but because they knew that Tommy Lee had been working on the thing for two weeks, and here he was trying to pass it off as a burst of inspiration. When he was done, there was a ripple of applause and some mumbles about how nice it was. He folded it and gave it to Don Schmidt "to put on the bulletin board in case anyone had a mind to copy it."

Then Schmidt got up and was brief and unexpectedly funny,

alluding to the "Great Programmer in the Sky" and hoping that a "little bit" of fondness for Pennington Inc. would remain in his computer. Tommy Lee allowed it would.

Then there was silence. No one, not one more of the forty-plus, had anything he or she wanted to say. It was embarrassing. Tommy Lee leaned across Harold Patterson, who was tipped back, smoking, and whispered to Arnie Jax. There was more silence. Then, as the rustle that previews departure started up, Jax said something inaudible to Tommy Lee, who answered: "If you've a mind to." Jax stood up.

"Before you leave, before we let this guy go away, I think there is something you ought to know. On July Fourth, in Washington, the President will confer the Congressional Medal of Honor on him, commemorating twenty years later the bravery he showed in Vietnam. I just thought you ought to know the kind of person we've had in our midst these past few years." And he reached over and shook Tommy Lee's hand.

And Tommy Lee burst into tears. "You blew me away there, Jaxie. Just blew me away." And he walked quickly from the hall to compose himself. When he returned, everyone was headed toward the door. A few had quizzical expressions: what was this Medal of Honor shit? For many of them it was the last time they would lay eyes on him. For all of them it had been a nice couple of hours, and when they stepped outside they found the sun burning and the snow melting. Most of the men didn't bother to put their overcoats on.

And now it's all over. The rest of his belongings have been thrown into a cardboard box. He had taken off his sport coat in anticipation of a bunch of people coming down to shoot the crap with him, but everyone had gone back to work. It is as though he'd already gone. Zola, Kerouac, even Arnie Jax, wander through his office, find what they want, and walk out with hardly a word.

"Well," Tommy Lee says, hoisting himself up out of the chair, "I guess maybe I'll just get myself out of here," and for the last time he hawks into his Styrofoam cup, which he absentmindedly leaves on the desk.

He sees Jax passing by the door and waves him in.

"I'm gettin' on, good buddy. Thanks for what you said back there."

"For nothing. You take care of yourself. We'll be in touch."

"Tell everyone I'll be missin' 'em."

"Will do. Will do."

They shake hands and Jax closes the door to the computer room behind him, leaving Tommy Lee on the outside. Tommy Lee bundles into his sport coat, tosses his overcoat over his shoulder, cradles the cardboard box to his chest, and slowly climbs the stairs.

In exactly one hour and fourteen minutes, Jake Henchard will retire, bringing to a close twenty-two contented years in the back shop of Pennington Inc. Jake is one of the two men Gerry Hanrahan had promised would be leaving within a couple of months.

Jake Henchard is special. In a group of very decent, reasonably hardworking people, Jake stands out as all that and much more. In such a homogenized congregation, Jake rises like cream to the top. The reason is simple: Jake gives a damn about the people around him and he is always willing to go that extra step to make sure that people around him know they can count on it.

Jake is no Boy Scout. There have been some rough-and-tumble times in his life, in which the other guy did not come out the better for having met up with Jake. And he is not a "preachin'" man trying to jam goodness and mercy down everyone's throats. No, it's just that Jake has a working theory that, as he says, "It's easier to like someone than to dislike them," and you have to be downright perverse to dislike someone who is determined to like you, regardless.

Jake is one of the three maintenance men. There isn't much around the plant Jake hasn't put his hand on at least once over the years. On balance, there isn't much he does very well. As a mechanic, he is average. He will be replaced with no material loss to the company. What is irreplaceable is that rare facility for being unflappable in any situation. Nothing excites Jake, nothing makes him mad. Nothing is impossible unless it is something that has to be done yesterday. That is when he shakes his huge head and politely suggests to his boss that maybe Mike or Dave better take a shot at it.

He is presently making his way along the floor, saying his private good-byes. Sixty-five years old and hardly an ounce of fat on him. A tough man, but gentle. Still, if Jake asks you to do something you were inclined against, you might do well to say, "Gladly." For Jake is imposing. His smooth, nearly bald dome is almost always covered by a dark blue wool cap. His ears are large, stand out a bit, and appear to have been boxed a few times. His face is both serene and tired, leathery and well lined. His eyes are blue and edged deeply with crow's-feet. His neck is long and sturdy, the back hatch-marked by time and sun, reflective of long hours on his farm tractor in the haying sun. His shoulders are square and muscular. His stomach is flat. He dresses in dark work clothes and generally wears a gray T-shirt beneath. And he has huge, gnarled, Thunder-of-Thor hands, thick and calloused. It is the hands that convey his authority.

"Hello, Chico," Jake says to Antonio Silva of "heat treat," who is squaring off a set of granulator knives. "Chico and the man. Where's the man, Chico?" He tucks a little punch into Antonio's stomach. "A nice little Chico growing in there?"

"Go fuck yourself, old man," Antonio answers, smiling. When Antonio first started with the company four years ago, there were no Portuguese in either the front office or the back shop. There were also no Puerto Ricans, although Puerto Ricans make up a large part of the local population. There was some feeling about Puerto Ricans, however, and those with the feelings made no distinction between the Portuguese and the

Puerto Ricans. It was Jake Henchard who had gone up to Antonio and pulled the "Chico and the man" line on him and gave him the friendly tap in the gut to let him know he had a friend. When the hat came by for Jake's farewell kitty, Antonio tucked a five-dollar bill in it.

"She goin' better now, Dick?"

"Surer'n hell. You done a good job, Jake."

Last week, K-6, the grinding machine, wouldn't bring the knives in close enough for the grindstones to put on the final bevel. Jake spent the better part of the day snaking filings out of the bed where they had compacted over the years. It had meant stretching his old body at an awkward angle and reaching in with coat hangers and easing the stuff out in dribs and drabs. By the end of the day his knuckles were raw and bloody and saturated with cutting oil. His back ached almost as badly as it had twenty-five years earlier when he'd had to give up driving 'dozers because of the way they tossed him around.

If Dick had cleaned the machine . . . but who has time to be cleaning machines, or who even knows how, or cares to know how? For $7.52 per hour Pennington Inc. gets someone who will affix a precut, welded, and rolled steel bar on a magnetized carriage, will set the angle of the grinding wheels according to the specifications, will set the timer, push the button, and will stand there, listening to his radio, every so often checking progress, until the bell rings and it is time to unload and repeat. For the aforementioned sum, this person will do this eight hours a day, five days a week, time off for holidays, vacations, and, of late, for layoffs and shutdowns. They will do this and no other job. Union rules. Cleaning the machine is not part of the contract.

You can't call the work Jake did on K-6 a favor. It was his job. It was the way he did it, the good spirit, the earnestness. It was a grunt's job and somehow Jake imbued it with . . . dignity. And as he wanders around, not even making a pretence of working on this last day, he is reaping the rewards due someone who never found the menial beneath him, who quietly assumed that everyone was walking down the same road and, what the hell, anything you could do to help the other guy along probably wouldn't hurt you, might help him.

". . . and when I get home early, here is a package for me from my daughter, the nurse that lives in Tampa?"

Wood shop foreman John Genest has stopped to shake Jake's hand and wish him the best. Jake naturally asked about John's wife, who has just gone under the knife for the twenty-first time in four years, and so on until the subject of Jake's recent birthday party came up and Jake knew that John would appreciate this little story:

". . . so I opens it and right on top is a letter, which I open, and it says that she knows me and the Mrs. aren't going to do anything special because we never do, and so we got to follow her instructions just the way she's got them.

"In the box there's all these things wrapped up pretty and all of them is numbered so we got to start with '1.' Which is a cake mix . . . '2' is a frosting mix . . . '3' is two of them paper placemats with candles around the edge and 'Happy Birthday' across where the plate goes . . . then there's two sets of plastic knives and forks . . . and two paper plates and a couple of cups . . . and a package of lemonade . . . and finally there's two hats and two of them things you blow on and the end goes shooting out . . . and she was right. We didn't have plans to go out."

"Jake, I can't figure why she'd do such a nice thing for someone as ornery as you, but then, there's a lot of things I can't figure. So what's new?"

Jake's moment has arrived — on the men's, not the company's time. Big Herman Polan, the maintenance supervisor, is standing, arms akimbo, by the old green lockers in the Numerical Control Room. Another cigarette is hanging from his lips and he is softly coughing as the smoke flows steadily out his nose. An ash grows and begins to dangle. Big Herman has a manila folder under his left arm. He is smiling kindly at the men as they gather around, but he doesn't say anything.

There is the constant din of the machines, although this diminishes rapidly as, one after another, they are shut down for the noon lunch break. The men chat amongst themselves. Frequently a "thclunk" is heard as a man punches out.

Jake is standing across the informal circle from Big Herman. Building 1 supervisor Bud Darcy has joined him, as has union treasurer Pat Loren.

"I guess we can get things started here," Big Herman rasps. There is silence among the forty or so men who have gathered. "In my thirty years with this company it has been my pleasure to deal with some very fine and wonderful people, each of whom in his own way has made a real contribution to Pennington Inc. And I am proud to be here today to say 'thank you and good-bye' to as fine a man, as fine a gentleman, as we have ever had the pleasure of having among us.

"Jake, if you would come forward, I would like to give you this certificate of the company's appreciation for the contribution you have made in the twenty-two years you have been with us. . . . Thank you, Jake, and the best of luck in your retirement. I have the feeling you will not be bored."

There is a round of loud and heartfelt applause and some laughter. Boredom is the lurking menace that faces the majority of the men who muster out of the back shop. It's what keeps them around, and later coming back to visit. Everyone is jealous of Jake and his farm.

"And I nearly forgot," Big Herman adds. "Here is a little something to help you over your first week without us: $156 from the men around you."

More applause and a couple of whistles. One hundred fifty-six dollars is a good purse, the average being around $115.

"And before you run off to spend that, Jake," Pat Loren booms over the applause, "here is your union retirement card and a check for $150. Good luck."

And that is it.

Jake stands there and says "thank you" a few times. One by one the men come up and shake his hand, and leave for lunch. In a matter of minutes Jake Henchard is alone. He follows the last man out the door and makes his way to the far parking lot. By tradition, the company gives the retiree the afternoon off.

The next departure was less ceremonious than the previous two.

On a Wednesday, about a month and a half after Tommy Lee McRainey's farewell party, about three weeks after the back shop said good-bye to Jake Henchard, about four days after he had given his notice, Dan Hutton told executive secretary Natalie Spangler to go fuck herself, or at least that is what Natalie swore as she crashed into Bart's office demanding redress.

Here is what supposedly happened, but first some background.

One of the first moves that Gerry Hanrahan had made upon taking over Manufacturing was to eliminate the Industrial Engineering Office, giving early retirement to Dick Trout, who at fifty-eight had been with Pennington Inc. for twenty-eight years. It had been a blow to the department, a shock to many of the old-timers in the front office, and an early signal from Hanrahan that loyalty ran a distant second to efficiency.

This left Industrial Engineering's headquarters, known out in the yard as "the little red schoolhouse," empty. Purchasing was eventually moved into it. Hutton appreciated this decision, for it meant that he could at last move his immaculate BMW off Beauchamp Street and put it safe and sound in the back lot next to the "little red schoolhouse." Or so Hutton thought. Unhappily, it didn't mean anything of the sort, for although parking spaces are not assigned officially, they are possessed de facto, and, unwittingly, Hutton had usurped Natalie Spangler's.

Perhaps if Natalie had been in a better mood, Hutton's recently announced departure would have been more gently paced. He had not been with the company long enough to have deserved his own party; still, people would have had a chance to drift up to him in the hall and wish him well. But in the middle of the night, Natalie's father had been taken to the Suffolk Memorial Hospital with a minor heart attack — his third in a year — and Natalie admitted later that she was "bouncing off walls." Hutton's trespass was something tangible to spend her worries on. She got on the phone immediately and ordered him to move that car.

The absurdity of what was to follow was not lost on him. For two years he had parked his car practically on the front doorstep, and no one had ever mentioned it. Now he had parked it off the road, out of everybody's way, and here was this crazy lady (whom he didn't hold in much esteem anyway) ordering him (not asking, no "pleases") to stop whatever he was doing and move it. It didn't take Hutton long to be standing in front of Natalie's desk.

According to Hutton, all he'd done was ask her why he had to move the car. Her explanation was "Because I told you to." After a couple of minutes of trying to render her more explicit, Hutton says he asked: "What the fuck do you want?"

According to Natalie, he came in and told her he wasn't about to move anything. She told him he had to. He then told her to "go fuck herself."

Both agree the word *fuck* was used. The chances are that, given Natalie's state of mind, any word would have sufficed, although Hutton concedes that *fuck* was probably a poor choice. At any rate, before he knew what had happened, he was in Bart's office, and three minutes later, he was on his way — to the little red schoolhouse to clean out his desk (which he'd only just filled up three days earlier), and twenty minutes later he was headed through the gates, the company rapidly disappearing in his rearview mirror, an unexpected vacation awaiting him.

For her part, the purge of Hutton proved a weak cathartic, and Natalie left at noon and didn't bother to return until the following day.

7

Blueprints for Change

★

Rick Carney of Engineering and Gerry Hanrahan of Manufacturing have a lot in common. Both are bright, aggressive, not quite middle-aged engineers who have opted for management over the drawing board.

There are some differences. Hanrahan is already a vice-president (Carney only supervises the department's three draftsmen). He also has not spent all his working life at Pennington Inc. Of all the differences, that is the most telling.

It is only coincidence, thought not particularly surprising, that on this Tuesday in February, at opposite ends of the long hall through the front office, Gerry and Rick, each on his own, are trying to explain how the place works; and both, being engineers, have transferred their observations and wonderments to blueprints. The only major difference is that Hanrahan is in a position to pay a consultant ten thousand dollars to help him, and Carney has prepared his work unsolicited, by himself, and for the most part on his own time.

There is one other difference. When they are done, Hanrahan can do something about changing things. Carney can't.

Down in Engineering, Rick Carney is standing before an empty draftsman's table. In front of him is a sheet of drafting paper. It is taped down and Rick is drawing horizontal, vertical, and diagonal lines, some of which intersect, some of which stand free, waiting for a connection, if Rick can figure out where.

The specific inspiration for this burgeoning schema is a

memo which he has tacked to the upper right-hand side of the table. The memo is dated "Feb 3"; to "P. D. Bourassa"; from "R. W. Markham"; "Subject: Railac 18″ Cuber"; and it states, in substance, that the customer in question wants a change and has paid for it.

Carney is not upset by the message. What concerns him is the "cc" (carbon copies) list at the bottom left of the memo. There are no fewer than nine initials affixed, and Rick cannot bring himself to accept that this limited message needs to be brought to the attention of nine people over and above the two principals.

"That is Goddamned inefficient," Rick had grumbled the first time he'd seen the memo. "Any system that breeds this sort of thing isn't any damned system at all and should be gotten rid of."

Which is undoubtedly true. It was certainly a far cry from operating off the backs of envelopes, Rick remembered thinking, recalling Schmidt's "sense of urgency" speech. But what is the system that does breed this sort of thing? Only last week did it occur to him that for sixteen years he had accepted whatever it was, from time to time cursed it, but clearly had absorbed it without having any idea of how it worked. So he got out the paper and started drawing lines.

What he really wanted to see — and it was to actually see it that he was drawing — were the lines of responsibility. Why was it necessary that eleven people had to be privy to information as limited, as trivial as that carried in the memo? He had studied the initials and had asked himself: why does this guy have to know that? In answering the question he'd first had to review what each person's job was in the company, what area of the total business he was responsible for — and how responsible. He'd discovered there was an awful lot of overlap, if not outright duplication, and, worse, waste. It was with trepidation — if he had not truly loved the company he would have stopped there and gone back to doing what he was paid to do

— he began to outline the hierarchical setup of Pennington Inc.

He started top center with "Chairman of the Board." Directly below he wrote: "President" and connected the two with a short line. As far as he knew, Don Schmidt reported to Frank Pennington. He then isolated the six vice-presidents, giving all equal space horizontally, connecting them all with a straight line across the sheet, with a vertical line dead center up to "President." Next, he listed below each vice-president the names of all the respective supervisors, their areas of responsibility, and below this, the names of all the employees under each supervisor. It seemed like the easiest and most logical way to get everybody situated. The trouble was, when he started to draw lines showing some of the flow of authority, he realized that there were either too many Indians or too many chiefs. He couldn't decide which. Lines intersected at odd spots. People were informing others too early or too late and, most remarkably, there didn't appear to be anyone who was charged with knowing what was supposed to be happening at any given time. It was like a giant game of bumper cars. Chaos screamed up at him from the sheet.

He took a red pen and drew a line of red dots from a point between "vice-president" and "supervisor" across the page, linking Administration with Marketing, and in the middle he wrote "General Manager" and put in a connecting line of dots to "President" above.

It was at that moment that Rick Carney comprehended the ease with which systems grow obese in the course of being streamlined. His simple solution to an obvious problem seemed perfectly reasonable: if there had to be so much interdepartmental communication, while at the same time each department was charged with so many diverse responsibilities that it could scarcely keep tabs on all the projects underway, then the introduction of one person to coordinate everything was the only plausible solution. Except that the more he thought about it, the less sense it made, and he realized that all he had accomplished was the addition of another set of initials to sit under "cc."

He had rolled the sheet up and stuck it between the wall and his desk, and had gone home and not looked at it for nearly three weeks. Then yesterday he'd heard that an office furlough was about to go into effect, and that sometime in the next three weeks he would be obliged to take a week off, free of pay, compliments of the recession (and the "ccs," he suspected).

"What perfect timing!" he'd cursed. The very time he'd planned to go to the Hyattsville National Bank and get a loan, so that he could start ordering materials for the house by Clear Lake that he and Julie had been planning for years and that was to get under way in June.

"What are we going to do?" Julie had asked.

"I'm going down and tell 'em I work for Pennington Inc., a good solid, smart company where I've been for half my life. I'll tell 'em that. What else am I going to do?" Rick had answered.

Seriously, what else was there to do? Get angry and try to bracket out the possibility that the company you'd spent maybe your best years with just might be half-assed, and that you probably should have gone looking around for something better when you'd been younger and worth something in the marketplace?

That had been last night's conversation and, later, his insomniac thoughts. Which was why Rick is standing in front of the drawing board again, staring at the sheet.

"Hopeless," he grumbles, untapes it, and rolls it up again, this time shoving it completely out of sight under his desk.

Down the hall, in the conference room, Gerry Hanrahan is unveiling the fruits of his labors, thumbtacking a series of large white sheets of paper to the near wall. The sheets are designed to demonstrate work flow in Manufacturing. The first two feature many blue lines leading to and from many small boxes in which are printed names. There are quite a few boxes, but there are three to four times as many blue lines, weaving hither and yon, creating the illusion of a design for a wooden-hulled sailboat. One sheet is for "capital goods" (the Marston Mixer, the Whirlwind, and the like), the other for "wear (knives) parts," the two manufacturing thrusts of Pennington Inc. The third sheet has fewer boxes and far fewer lines. This is Hanrahan's proposed solution to the mazes implied by the first two sheets.

There is an oppressive silence in the room. The full executive body is there. Each knows what Hanrahan is going to say, and no one is interested in hearing it. Hanrahan knows that everyone knows, and knows how they feel, but such is the reputation and power he has built up in such a short period that he doesn't care. He has determined that they are going to hear everything in as much detail as he can get away with. He is no longer the polite, inofficious "new boy." He now knows too much; he has looked around at all those who have been sidetracked by the hospitable Pennington Inc. sense of business, and he has realized that the only way to keep from pulling over and joining them is to fight and kick, and to make sure that his hand is always on something solid that he himself has constructed. (It has also begun to dawn on him that there might be more than just a future at Pennington Inc. One of these days the place might just be up for grabs, and he knows he is looking good.)

Today he is about to try something that has not been attempted very often in the past. He is going to tell people what he is doing and why. Theoretically this is called letting the right hand know what the left is up to, and it is his response to the often-grumbled complaint that all the departments are little fiefdoms operating autonomously, constantly confronting each other with faits accomplis, the end result being a pigpile with arms and legs sticking out in all directions and not very much being accomplished. Except some bruised feelings. Which pass in time and leave uncorrected the reasons the feelings were

73

bruised to begin with: namely, no one knows what the hell is going on, because many of the lines needed for communication have either never been connected, or never established in the first place.

The company may have lasted more than seventy-five years, but that should not immediately imply that its ways of doing business have either been right or particularly successful. Someone taught to accelerate with the left foot and clutch with the right can get the car down the road, as long as the way is fairly clear. Still, that is not how a car is to be driven — a discovery made in emergencies, and often too late.

There has been a lot of left-footed acceleration at Pennington Inc., primarily because in the course of three generations of self-taught Penningtons, ways were established that have not been altered or updated in decades. Like the buildings that house them, bodies have been added to fill real or imagined needs — and have not been discarded when the needs disappeared. The result is a confounding snarl of lines of responsibility, duty, communication that make students of contemporary (some grumble "textbook") management like Gerry Hanrahan wonder how anything ever got out the door.

And all the while, everyone imagines that what he is doing is how it is done elsewhere. It has taken the threat of bankruptcy, the presence of "company doctor" H. Edwin Blatchford, and the efficiency of Gerry Hanrahan to bring Pennington business-as-usual into perspective.

Hanrahan is no longer asking permission or soliciting advice. He will do what he has to — or what he thinks he has to — and the way he has read the situation, there isn't anyone around with the power to tell him he can't. And he is right. Everyone, including Schmidt, is either scared or awed by him. The guy is a front-rank professional manager with a seemingly uncanny knack for sizing up situations instantly and then being able to act definitively. Not that he is a gunslinger. Since the day he arrived, he has worked from seven in the morning until ten at night at least three days a week, from seven till eight P.M. two more, and always half a day on Saturday. And he has not been jawboning by the mailroom or the coffee machine. He has sat at his desk and slowly and methodically milled the grist from all the minds around him. Old-time employees like Gene Scola have been queried for hours at a time on what they know, and especially about whom: who can work, who can't, who can learn, who won't; who is essential, who expendable.

As far as Hanrahan is concerned, what has to be done is far less important than who is going to do it. The first piece of advice Don Schmidt gave him was: "Assemble your own team, hire your own people. Make them loyal to you and no one else, and you will survive here." In theory, Schmidt was right; in practice, untimely, for the company soon began laying people off in droves. Hiring a new staff was not one of Hanrahan's options. The trick was to take the staff he'd inherited from Bart and wean them away from Bart by whipping them into his kind of shape.

A cursory study of the company's own "Individual Merit Rating and Salary Planning Schedule" suggests that the material Hanrahan had to shape was average at best. The schedule not only lists the respective salaries of all the salaried and clerical personnel in the company, but also the performance rating of each as handed down by each supervisor, who himself was rated by his superior. Only the three Penningtons and Don Schmidt escaped the list.

There are three grades ranging from Acceptable (A) through Satisfactory (S) to Outstanding (O). There is no grade for Unsatisfactory. Of the eighty-one front office employees assessed, forty-three were marked A, thirty-five S, and only three O. Put another way, less than four percent were considered front rank, less than fifty percent were judged OK or better, and over fifty percent were thought to be — acceptable. The entire Finance department was A, as were half the top company officers. One of the O's went to the engineer brought in specifically to shepherd one machine, the Marston Mixer. Paradoxically, the sales

75

manager assigned only to that machine received a bare A. The remaining O's went to Tommy Lee McRainey, the departed head of Data Processing, and executive secretary Natalie Spangler.

As for the Manufacturing department, the area of greatest interest to Hanrahan, there were no O's, thirteen S's, and sixteen A's. In addition, the average tenure was over fifteen years. The department Hanrahan inherited from Bart was entrenched with layers of "family," and the single most effective weapon he had with which to motivate them was fear. He let it be known early on that the livelihood of a lot of long-time company servants lay in the hands of a professional manager whose own loyalty extended no farther than the job he held at that given point in time. There are no memories to blind Hanrahan. If the part doesn't — or won't — fit, he'll heave it and find a replacement.

"Thank you, Don, for giving me this time. Over the past month or so, as some of you are aware, we've been doing a study to try and find out how things really get done here. The answer is, I think, surprisingly well, considering. And the reason lies in the length of time most of our people have been here. No job description exists. There are no stated procedures, which means that no one could just come in off the street and do the job. It is my belief that, while it works, this is inefficient and calls out to be streamlined."

Hanrahan pauses to reach down to the table for a large binder, which he flips open. He is seemingly oblivious, or maybe impervious, to the cold, somewhat distracted looks on Frank, Harold, and Bart Pennington's faces. In the space of a couple of minutes, young Hanrahan has told them that the way they have been going about things for the past seventy-seven years is — how can it be put any other way? — stupid. And now they have to sit and listen. It is tantamount to being pilloried.

Hanrahan picks up a yardstick and takes a deep breath.

76

"We'll start with a customer purchase order which comes to us by mail.

"First, a copy goes to Sue and an original to Gene." (He traces two blue lines to two boxes.) "Sue adds the copy to the daily list, which she types, making a copy for Gene and sending the original to Sales for distribution. White order copies are given to Gene for review and he in turn forwards these on to Sales Administration. Customer purchase order copies are forwarded to Sales.

"Gene compares white orders to quote information, reviews purchase orders, and forwards originals to Fritzie. Fritzie receives white orders with description, researches existing item numbers and descriptions for similar knives, establishes print number and lists on steno pad, requests similar knife drawing from Engineering, enters new item number and description in notebook, and forwards to Dolores.

"Dolores completes customer order data entry form — for which there are nine separate steps — and returns the orders to Fritzie.

"Fritzie makes out our Quickie-Note — an eight-step process — and gives this to Angie, who creates the stock order or manufacturing order, a five-step process, and returns the Quickie-Note to Fritzie. If the quantity on hand cannot satisfy the requirement, Fritzie marks an 'M' on the Quickie-Note, signifying a manufacturing order is required. A 'manufacturing order' has nineteen steps, which, as you can see, involve not only more exchanges between Fritzie, Dolores, and Angie, but also include Betty Ann, Louise, Rick Carney, and Gene Scola . . ."

Hanrahan pauses for a second, resting the yardstick on the floor like a cane, and carefully surveys everyone around the room. "Company doctor" H. Edwin Blatchford, seated to his right, does the same thing.

". . . and I have only just begun. There are twenty-four pages here, and we are talking about one order for a set of knives. I submit to you that there is every reason to be proud we don't lose or mess up more orders than we do. And you are all aware, we do mess up.

"We are in the midst of making some changes, and what I have up here" (he taps the third chart) "is just one possible solution. As you can see, it is greatly simplified — and requires far fewer people. It depends in large part on accessing the computer better, and I am in constant touch with Arnie Jax about what we need. He is being very helpful. I would estimate that when we are ready to implement a new system, I will be able to reduce my staff by no less than two, maybe as many as four people.

"That's about all I have right now. Are there any questions?"

"How much did all that stuff cost us?" Harold Pennington asks, fidgeting with a sheath of papers in his lap.

"It'll be close to ten thousand by the time we're through," Hanrahan answers without elaboration.

"We had a study done back in the early sixties. The same sort of thing. Why'd we have to do another one and waste all that money?"

"The other one was outdated. This one will save the company the ten thousand and then some, I can guarantee you."

"I still think it's a waste. Have we paid the guy?"

Hanrahan nods, smiling politely as Harold shakes his head while staring coldly at Schmidt.

"If there are no more questions . . . Don, it's yours."

The men get up and leave the room. Only H. Edwin Blatchford stops on his way, turns around, looks Hanrahan in the eye, and says: "Good job."

Hanrahan waits until the room is empty before slowly, methodically unpinning the charts.

8

The Blatchford Report

★

On the final Friday of February, H. Edwin Blatchford delivered his official report on the state of the company. The presentation took place in the PRC conference room, late in the afternoon. All seven trustees attended. These included the three Penningtons, Don Schmidt, Edgar R. Worthley, Bart's brother-in-law, and the presidents of two similar-sized manufacturing companies, both located out of town. There were also two representatives from the First City Bank.

The meeting lasted three hours and consisted of a detailed description of the company's manifold problems, as listed in an outline provided by Blatchford to each of the trustees. The meeting was closed. In fact, it was not until late the following Monday morning that most people even knew it had taken place. At that time copies of the outline were made available to the vice-presidents, who then met with both Schmidt and Blatchford, who spelled out in detail just how each department was expected to respond. The first task — start cutting expenses.

Few, if any, copies of the outline made their way to the middle management ranks, although no specific effort was made to keep the contents classified. The accepted explanation for such confidentiality in a company in which office secrets are community fare is: "Anyone here could have written it."

What the report said in essence, was: "This company is running out of control." And while it stopped short of declaring the illness terminal, the implication was there: either get the oper-

79

ation in hand, which meant performing the kind of severe surgery that historically cut across Pennington grain, or plan on losing the company in the very near future.

After softening the blow with the observation that he had worked with companies whose fates had been more dire and that had remained afloat after judicious jettisoning, Blatchford ran through his conclusions:

"Inasmuch as there is no cost system, it is impossible for the company to know where it is going or what it is doing. While there is adequate reporting of expenses by many cost centers, there is no control over what is being spent and to which product the expenses apply.

"There are no budgets, so each department cannot be held accountable for what it spends.

"It is virtually impossible to determine where the company is making or losing money by product.

"The Marketing department is organized to handle sales of at least twice those of the company. This apparently is necessary because of the many varied markets the company tries to service. None of the sales of these markets are large enough to justify the expense.

"Many of the markets are declining without adequate products being in place to fill the gaps.

"Because sales are declining, the costs have increased, making some products noncompetitive.

"In 1981, nearly fifty percent of the company's gross margin was for marketing expense.

"Overhead costs in Manufacturing are extremely high. With the decline in heavy equipment, the high overhead will be too much to carry. However, Gerry Hanrahan appears to be capable and should be able to trim costs.

"The majority of Engineering's time is spent on Marston Mixer problems. Essentially no time is spent on new products. The cost of this department should be taken into account when determining the future of the Marston Mixer.

"Data Processing is a long way from putting out information necessary for management to run the company. There seems to be a concerted effort to get the basic material into the system, but results are a long way off. When it gets running, it will help but not solve the problems.

"There appears to be a lack of cohesiveness among the management group. When asked, who do you work for, much hedging. There are no guidelines on authority. People seem to do what they want. There is no decision-making process. The company does not have its people under control. It must be made clear to everybody who is running the company, and all others must respect his authority."

Blatchford's voice seemed to increase in volume as he addressed that last point. Bart and Harold nodded in agreement. Frank stared at the table, eyes almost closed. Don Schmidt almost grinned.

The following week, H. Edwin Blatchford, long-since nicknamed "Mr. What's-It-Cost," sat behind his desk in the former treasurer's office overlooking the PRC parking lot. With his coat off and his sleeves rolled up, he looked much like a professor who has just passed out a final exam and is now waiting for the students to go to work on it. And although the stakes were both real and high, the students were confused by an urge, on the one hand, to do well and please the professor and, on the other, to avoid facing the whole thing altogether.

For Blatchford had clearly stated that business-as-usual had not been working for a long time, was not working at the moment, and would not be acceptable in the future. Roughly translated, that meant that paternalism, "family spirit" friendship over efficiency — in effect, everything that made Pennington Inc. a warm, secure place to work in — must be rigorously examined and, if found to be in the way of good business practice, must be excised without a tear.

Gerry Hanrahan was excused from doing the exam because he was already well ahead of Blatchford.

Willis Farnsworth was tacitly exempted because his research expenses were the most meager of any department and his return on investment at least canceled them out.

Controller Roy Fitzgerald sat down and produced a long list of "cash conservation" ideas he thought would pare costs and lend black to the bottom line. Fitzgerald was secretly doing work similar to Blatchford's for a company in Canada and was frankly jealous of the impact Blatchford had made on the company. Fitzgerald maintained to anyone who would listen that he had explained in detail to Schmidt, a year ago, most of the things Blatchford had just "revealed," and that he had been called a Cassandra and shunted aside with Farnsworth.

When Fitzgerald presented his list to Blatchford, H. Edwin thanked him and set it on the far corner of his desk, then went back to pecking at his calculator. Fitzgerald stood there for a moment, waiting for some fraternal word. Finally he walked away and went back to his office and read the day's *Wall Street Journal.*

Doug Searles of Sales received in the mail a sample of the product he and Frank Patterson were desperately trying to encourage the Japanese to manufacture jointly. In light of the report, particularly Blatchford's ominous concerns over the real value of the Marston Mixer, which was integral to the project, Searles hurriedly raced the sample to Blatchford's office.

"I think you ought to see this. It came in the morning mail, like a good omen," Searles said confidentially to Blatchford, whom he privately considered an old fart with superannuated ideas of economics. He set the sample down on the desk between the calculator and Blatchford's right hand.

"It seems to Frank and me to be even better than we'd have thought it'd be. We're both real enthused about it, and from what we can gather from the Japs, they're tickled pink."

Searles carried on in this vein for over three minutes, words of praise, of exuberance tumbling over one another like young lambs in the early spring sun.

Blatchford held up the sample, turned it around and around very slowly, unexpressively, then handed it back to Searles.

"It looks goods. It might be something to pursue, but you haven't got half enough numbers yet," he said. "I've got to know what the real costs are going to be, what the guarantees are, what the commitment."

Like Fitzgerald the day before, Searles remained standing beside Blatchford's desk even though H. Edwin had returned to his calculator. He could not believe he was being sent back to his desk. In his three years with Pennington Inc., no one had ever dismissed *him* that way. He didn't like it, and he vowed it would not happen again.

The following Friday afternoon, Bart Pennington walked into Don Schmidt's office to return a printout Schmidt had given him to study earlier in the day. Schmidt was leaning back in his chair, coat off, tie knot pulled down, shirt collar button undone. One leg was crossed over the other. He was beaming like a new father.

Leaning against the windowsill, one arm draped over the row of books that sat on top of the old cast-iron radiator, his coat off, tie down, shirt collar unbuttoned, was H. Edwin Blatchford. He too was smiling, avuncularly.

Schmidt burst into laughter.

"Bart, you know what I was just saying to Edwin here, about how it's hard to believe, no sooner do I get appointed CEO [chief executive officer] than my first act is to sign a ten percent salary cut for myself."

Bart does not attempt to share in Schmidt's mirth. He is well aware of the salary cut, as it also extends to him, Frank, and Harold, but not to Searles or Hanrahan, both of whom make twenty thousand dollars a year more than he.

"That's something," Bart says laconically. "Nice weekend," he adds with grace and walks out the door.

Schmidt is clearly oblivious to Bart's chilliness. He is feeling so good. For he has been convinced all week that Blatchford's report has vindicated him and pointed the finger where he feels it should be, at Frank Pennington. As evidence of his conclusion, the board of trustees had met in special session on Wednesday afternoon and voted unanimously that he and no other was in charge. Frank had sent a memo to that effect to all departments, officially removing himself from all daily operations, taking responsibility only for foreign dealings. If he could have, Schmidt would have skipped and danced down the halls.

As for Blatchford, all he will do is smile. As far as he is concerned, his orchestration of the trustees' endorsement (only Schmidt considered it a promotion) is a test to see whether Schmidt can handle authority, if everyone else takes his hands off it. If he can't . . .

9

Enter the Back Shop

★

"**P**rofessor" Dicky Mizell had no idea who H. Edwin Blatchford was, or any idea why he should be bothered with knowing. The Professor probably couldn't name half the top officers in the company. He's barely ever said a word to Frank or Harold. He'd nodded once to Don Schmidt and infrequently said "hello" to Bart. Hanrahan was only a name to him, Farnsworth a foreign buzz, and Searles?

But even before the layoff notice went on the bulletin board by the time clock, the Professor had known that something was up. Everybody in the back shop sensed it. They didn't know what shape it might take, but it was obvious a bell was knelling.

There was no work except make-work. Guys were standing around all day with their thumbs up their asses, trying to look occupied. But the way the Professor knew for sure was that he'd rattled through *The Second Deadly Sin* in a week, and it should have taken him two, even two and a half.

The Professor and his caches of paperbacks stuck in drawers throughout the packing room were a legend in the back shop. For ten years, five days a week, he had rolled himself out of his sagging bed at about three P.M., thrown some water on his face and thinning hair, stepped into a pair of old pants, stuck his arms through the sleeves of a worn shirt (in winter he'd leave time to button it), spread a couple of peanut butter and jelly sandwiches, and shuffled across the green to take his place at the packing table, as around him the day shift was punching out.

When times were good and there were a lot of knives going out the door, there would be overtime, and Hod and Steve would hold over for a couple of hours. Which used to annoy him. But they were all right, Hod and Steve. They stuck together, talked union business and niggers and spics — and golf . . . and golf. Still, they didn't bother the Professor much; and by six o'clock, they'd have cleared out, and then he'd have the place to himself.

He liked it solitary like that, without anyone coming around and asking what was doing and maybe taking you off the job and putting you off someplace, on something else you weren't supposed to do with your union classification. But the Professor did it, because what the hell. There wasn't no profit in being hard-assed like some of the boys, like Hod and Steve, who kept flashing the union contract all the time they was sitting on their haunches. No, the Professor liked being alone, where you could work your own pace and, if you wanted to take a break, you took one. You didn't ask no one and no one asked you why. If you had to have a job, this one in Packing beat hell out of digging graves or driving trucks. No hassle. A man could work right up to the Final Friday and not pay it much mind on the way.

Then, one day a month ago, for the first time since anyone could remember — and that included the "old ones," Carlo Orsini and Jimmy Ouellette — there was no second shift. Christmastime they'd killed the third shift, but that hadn't been much of a shift anyway and hadn't been in place long enough for anyone to take it into his skin. There weren't but twenty men on it. There had been a little "bumping," a little rearranging of jobs, but in general, the faces hadn't changed much. Most of the guys on the third shift hadn't accumulated much seniority and kind of disappeared without a trace or a ripple.

But killing the second shift, that was a different story. The second shift was a way of life for a lot of the guys. Their inner workings were timed to nights, not days. Forced to work days they were finding that they couldn't sleep when they were supposed to, and they were coming home tired and grouchy. Although many of them had once worked days and had been put on nights against their wills, most of them soon agreed they never wanted days again. Too much noise. Too much hustle. Too much hassling with the floor bosses. They were in shock.

The Professor was luckier than some of the other guys. He knew the packing room day shift — Hod, Steve, and Harve. Only Harve was leaving, because the Professor had had to bump him to get on days. It was too bad. He hated doing it, because Harve was good people. It worked out okay. Harve bumped Big Gordo in the yard. So the bump cost Harve a couple of bucks an hour in grade. At least they both had jobs. Twenty-five other guys had been bumped out to the street.

It was a helluva way to bring in the new year.

You'd think that with bodies disappearing on all sides of them that the men in the back shop would have been more concerned about their futures. They were not, and for a good reason: most of those being laid off were new and young and not part of the Pennington "family." For example, the Pennington Golf Team did not suffer a single casualty. A loss from its ranks might have gotten someone's attention.

What happened was that the more layoffs there were, the more things returned to the way they always had been. Before the Christmas cuts the back shop work force had stood at nearly one hundred and fifty and the average tenure was nine years. At Pennington Inc. the length of tenure yields an equal degree of loyalty. The less someone has been around, the more inclined he is to read adversity as a signal of doom. Conversely, the longer the tenure, the more willing one is to dismiss adversity as a passing phase. Consequently, the greater the attrition, the more widespread the confidence in the future of the company. After all, if you have worked for Pennington Inc. for over twenty years, as more than a third of the men have, if in fact you have been raised to Pennington Inc. because your father, your uncle, your older brother has worked there all his life, you have seen — or heard of — the good times and the bad; and you know for a fact that the company always survives and will never abandon you. The Penningtons know what the hell they are doing. They always have, always will. All you have to do is keep coming to work on time . . .

. . . like the Professor.

. . . like Tito Balboni, who has been coming to work on lathes for thirty-nine years. His heart has been giving him trouble over the last couple, and his friends have been suggesting he think of retiring. Every time he considers it he asks himself: "What'm I gonna do retired?" which translates into "What can I do besides work lathes?" And the frightening answer raises his blood pressure and he has to stop considering, just to spare his heart.

Tito is considered a good lathe operator, but he is best known for his obsession with lotteries. He calls this his hedge against inflation. You name the game, Tito has bought at least one ticket for it. Unhappily for him, his return on investment is low. He takes this in stride. In fact, he advertises the fact. Taped to his workbench are all the losing stubbs Tito has bought over the past few years:

— The Twenty-Four-Hour Game, The Big Money Game, Yankee Doodle Dollars, the Santa Claus Game, the New Hampshire Presidential Instant Game, the New Jersey State Lottery, the State of Michigan Lottery, the Maine State Lottery, the Instant Baseball Game, the Instant Football Game, The New $50,000 Match, the $1,000,000 TV Game, and Tic-Tac Dough. Twenty-four separate and distinct fortunes, all lost to someone else. From the look of his luck, the only game Tito stood a chance of winning was the Polish Lottery — "One million Dollars — a Dollar a Day for a Million Years."

. . . like Gregory Abajian. He has been with Pennington Inc. for only twenty-seven years, all of them on what is called the "boring mill." This is a huge upright lathe designed to perform only one function: the milling of both the interior and exterior of a large cast cone, which will ultimately be the mushing part of a pulp refining machine.

Gregory arrived at Pennington Inc. in 1955, coincident with the arrival of the boring mills. He started on them, he has never run any other machine, and if he and the company should live long enough, he will end his working life on them. Gregory is fifty-eight, and if he were to have his life to live over again, he says he might be more inclined to listen to Mother Abajian's early advice: "Whatever you do, Gregory, be sure you are your own boss."

Gregory says that when Mother Abajian was passing out free advice he was too young to appreciate its value. If he had not been, he thinks now he would have liked to have been an undertaker, because "I like to do things for people . . . and a good undertaker takes care of people during tough times." What Gregory is now, besides being a good boring mill operator, is a good nurseryman. People who have tried them say that Gregory's apples are the sweetest in the area. Sadly, Gregory once again failed to follow Mother Abajian's dictum. The orchard he carefully nurses belongs to his mother-in-law. She is very old and not well. It also stands just off the main street of a rapidly growing town. And when the old lady passes away, her family intends to sell it all for development, quickly.

"It's an old orchard. It should have been replanted," Gregory says, dolefully.

. . . like Carlo Orsini and Jimmy Ouellete over in the Numerical Control (NC) room, and Lyle Driscoll of the wood shop, and the "Hardy Boys," Jack Bodin and Al Martin, the grinders who every day for over twenty years have eaten their lunches together while walking briskly counterclockwise around the green.

. . . not quite like Henry Grandmaison in the machine shop. Henry is not one of those "sleepy old pops who" (he alleges) "haven't done a full day's work in the last twenty years . . . and who're going to die at their machines or while trying to get there . . . while young guys who want to work are out walking the streets looking."

Henry is a machinist first class, although he has been only three years with the company. The machinists are the company craftsmen, the only back shop employees who have to know what they are doing before they are hired to do it. When you apply for a machinist's position, you can't write down for work experience Dunkin' Donuts, Burger King, or Valley Building Center, which have frequently been the sole qualifications necessary for many currently operating the machinery in Building 1 and who like to bill themselves as machinists but are listed as machine operators.

Unlike the Professor, Tito, Gregory, and the others, Henry is young, self-motivated, and utterly unattached emotionally to the company. If the company should fold tomorrow, he would dispassionately collect his tools and walk out the gate without looking back. He cares for his family, his future, and, as far as Pennington Inc. is concerned, the task at hand, whatever it might be. Every evening he checks the Classifieds in the *Suffolk Times*, turning first to Help Wanted, just to see what is around; turning next to Miscellaneous, just to see if an industrial metal lathe has turned up — for himself.

For unlike Gregory Abajian, Henry is determined to be his own boss, eventually, and he has a plan. First, he must make enough money, which, he states, is why he works at Pennington Inc. while scouting the Help Wanteds. When he is ready, and opportunity strikes, he will buy his own lathe. When he has that lathe, he will find a small work space for it, maybe just a garage at first, and he'll take out an ad in the newspaper, get his phone number in the Yellow Pages, will quit working wherever he is, and will be his own man, his own boss.

That is Henry's plan. Every day for the past eight years, he has refined it, updated it. It is his preciously nurtured escape route, without which his life would seem a passage of eight-hour workdays and eight-hour sleepnights, with the only profit to show for his efforts being a lovely one-year-old princess whose baby pictures adorn the inside of his toolbox lid.

"Next spring, I think I'll be ready," he guesses. Like the "sleepy old pops" he so disdains, Henry can't really conceive that at Pennington Inc. "next spring" might be a long way off.

10

Heat Treat

★

I n response to the Blatchford Report, Marketing has prepared a "profile" of the company, which it is broadcasting
throughout various markets in hopes of attracting contract work
to ease overhead costs. The profile is understandably expan-
sive, emphasizing that "Pennington Inc.'s facilities, equipment,
and personnel provide technical expertise not often found in a
small business environment." It goes on to list all the company's
available equipment. The list takes up four pages. For example, there are:

- a Giddings & Lewis-Bickford 3-axis CNC "Numericenter-
  10HS" horizontal machining center with 24-tool automatic
  tool changer and 24" rotary table;
- a Mattison grinder;
- a Brown & Sharpe surface grinder;
- a Thompson crush form grinder;
- a Forges DeGilley horizontal boring mill;
- a Cincinnati "Hypowermatic" slab milling machine;
- a Whitcomb planer mill;
- a Broadbent-Schofield tracer lathe;
- a Jones & Lamson optical comparator.

The clear intent of the "profile" is to present Pennington Inc.
as a contemporary company with an up-to-date facility capable
of producing advanced work in a professionally current
manner.

The fact is, Pennington Inc. is a very old company with an aging facility, capable of producing relatively unsophisticated work in an increasingly outmoded manner. The work it does do, however, is of top quality, and when the profile suggests that its "excellent quality is respected around the world," it offers a boast of some substance.

What the company does best is what it has done the longest: the forging and forming of industrial knives. At one point in its recent history, the company offered over a thousand variations on its knives, each specifically designed or adjusted to meet customer demands in such diverse fields as the leather, the paper, the lumber, and the plastics industries. Pennington knives can be found in chippers that reduce entire trees for pulp; in shearing machines that lop off telephone books; in cutters that peel off veneers. These knives range from a foot long to four and five feet long, and are formed out of all manner of alloys and tempers, then finished often to fairly demanding tolerances.

But fundamental to the position knives play in the business is the "wear" detail, for Pennington Inc. not only fashions the original knife, it also repairs, rebuilds, and resharpens that knife over and over again, establishing a cycle that almost guarantees an annual renewal of business. Flomacs, Whirlwinds, and Marston Mixers sell once, return a single moment of profit, and add nothing more to the company's bottom line. Knives come back again and again, each time paying their way.

And for the past sixty-five years, all the knives have been made in Building 1, which is located on the other side of the wall from the front office. A large tin-covered sliding door stands at the entrance.

Building 1 is an aggregate of smaller buildings, the first erected in 1913, to which a mirror version was added in 1917. Throughout subsequent decades various additions and annexes have been accumulated. The result is a rambling, disjointed set of areas in which everything is touched with a fine oil-and-soot patina. A sooty bank of windows runs the length of the right, or train-track, side. Soot-covered windows and vents stretch the length of the peak. The concrete block walls are soot-gray, and much of the space the walls enclose is filled with machines.

Large, dark-green machines are numbered in yellow K-1, K-2, through K-13. There are some Ks missing — retired machines. When the men talk about them, they rarely refer to them as other than "that K-11 over there is leaking oil" or "I remember when they first got K-5. Bruno Baron's father was the first to work on her." You have to remind yourself that these are steel-cold objects, impervious to cajolery, incapable of returning kindnesses. Like boats, they are often referred to in the feminine, perhaps because men are the operators and many of these men have spent the better part of their lives with them, spent more waking time there than with their wives.

Routes between the heavy machinery are marked out in yellow lines. As late as the early forties, fifty-five-gallon drums used to stand at intersections. Wood fires were kept burning in them and that was the winter heat. Then is when men worked for a living, those around who can still remember will say. Then there were no radios as there are now, hanging from posts by the machine operators. Then there were no little coffeepots with the makings in lockers or on improvised shelves. Then there were probably calendar girls in the lockers, but no lottery sheets taped to the walls or the posts, recording the men's weekly numbers.

The atmosphere in Building 1 is laden with the constant drone of the large machines, with the permeating smell of cutting oil, with the blare of competing rock radio stations and the yelling of the men to one another over the noise of machines. What natural light there is seems spent from the effort needed to work through the miasma, and the artificial lights are naturally weak and random.

And cutting a swath across the middle of Building 1 is the

darkest, grimmest, grimiest area in the entire company. It is called "heat treat."

Heat treat is the starting gate for all the knives. It is here that they are cut to length, annealed, tempered, and generally prepared for shaping and sharpening. The area consists of a set of large ovens, splattered vats of orange molten lead, slick tanks of cooling oil, and, in the far corner to the left, two blast furnaces and an ancient, almost prehistoric, rolling mill.

Heat treat has been an integral part of production since the early twenties, when Frank's and Harold's father, S. R., had it installed. The intent then was to give the company as complete control over the quality of its knives as it could obtain. By borrowing techniques being developed in the growing auto industry, S. R. felt the company could adjust the properties in the steel to meet specific demands from various customers. Pennington Inc. was one of the first companies of its type and size to offer such a service, and even now the bulk of its repeat customers are carryovers from those earlier leadership days.

Heat treat is considered a hellhole and its denizens are on the lowest rung of the company ladder. It is the most physically demanding area in the back shop, which accounts for the high turnover, even in the worst of times. On the other hand, it is also the least boring area, so that it attracts a certain kind of broad-shouldered, independent, free-spirited (rowdy?) character, who takes the verbal abuse and the many burns as badges of courage. Old Carlo Orsini and Jimmy Ouellette of the NC room worked heat treat for over forty years, as they will gladly tell you.

The current crew is gathered by the rolling mill.

Dark goggles are tipped back, Steve McQueen–like, on their foreheads, and they are smoking away as though each had a wife in the throes of labor. These are the company "animals" — lead man Hack Harden, assistant lead man Antonio Silva, Antonio's little brother, Tony, former Air Force MP Rocko Robestelli, and "Fuck 'Em" William Baxter.

"The rolling mill" is the name given to the dimly lit area in the corner where the two forges stand. Once all knives passed through the rolling mill. Now some come prehardened and ready for cutting and sharpening. Some, however, large knives in particular, are made up of two steels, one very hard for the cutting edge, the other much softer for the "backing" or non-cutting half. The two metals are spot-welded edge to edge, then brought to the rolling mill, where they are fired nearly molten hot in the forges, then hammered and rolled out into long, unified bars. Thus, the rolling mill is the first major step in the manufacturing process.

When business is good, the mill is working in two shifts, five days a week. A sign of the current state of business is that this is the first time in over a week that the forges have been fired up.

Everyone except William Baxter is already exhausted, and the morning is still young. Hack is sitting on the edge of the cooling bucket that holds the tongs. Antonio is leaning on both elbows on the standup desk. Tony is backed against the butt edge of the wall that divides the rolling mill from the cutting room, his arms hanging limply at his side. And Rocko is seated on a skid of future granulator knives, his head in his hands, sweat pouring down his neck. And "Fuck 'Em" William Baxter is standing there, hands in pockets, not a drop of sweat on him, enjoying the break with the rest of the boys.

Of course William has scarcely done a lick of work since Hack and the rest began rolling out knives three hours ago. He has been futzing with the sandblaster and has tended to some knives being tempered in the oven. But every time he sees that Hack and the crew are not actually engaged in work, he stops whatever he's doing and comes over to stand with them.

"Fuck 'Em" William is fifty years old, stands approximately five feet three inches tall, is physically slight but hard, mentally lazy, verbally foul, punctuating all — that is, all — sentences with some variation of "fuck," and he appears to pass most of his time taking a break. William is one of those who fell from heaven when the second shift was disbanded, and he has had trouble adjusting to work in the daylight — or maybe just to working. They say about William that his "get-up-and-go" has "gotten up and gone." Like many Pennington Inc. employees, he is a legacy. His brother retired from the company in January after thirty-six years on K-6. He has a nephew in Quality Control. He also lives across the green in a one-bedroom apartment, which he shares with a current lady friend. And when he is not watching TV, he is around the corner at the Franco-American Ward 8 Club or over at the Elks. The perimeter of William Baxter's world is restricted. He is also considered too weak and, therefore, too great a risk, for the rolling mill, which is an image he has encouraged since "bumping" in. Which is why he alone is not sweating.

Hack Harden is the "lead man," which, in the order of things means that he is in charge of heat treat. He reports to foreman Walt Poirier, who reports to Building 1 supervisor Bud Darcy, who answers to Gerry Hanrahan, whose boss is Don Schmidt. Being lead man also means, according to the union contract, that he cannot be bumped.

Hack is ideally suited for heat treat. He has a gentle, relaxed temper, which infrequently takes unauthorized leaves of absence. At such times he yells and hollers and scares the hell out of everybody before relaxing back into the calm people expect of him. Hack is easy to work for, but is just unbalanced enough to be dangerous. So when Hack jumps up and says: "OK, men, let's get another one," the other three bodies spring into some form of action.

The first person to the tongs is Antonio Silva. Antonio is no bigger than "Fuck 'Em" William Baxter and probably no stronger, but Antonio has an immigrant's view of work in the United States, to wit: you work hard, you save your money, everything will be good. Whatever you do, don't cause no trouble. Consequently, Antonio is the first to get his silver asbestos gloves on, his dark goggles fixed to his nose, the tongs firmly gripped, his feet planted in the classic John L. Sullivan "dukes up" stance in front of the forge door.

The kid is tough, or at least that is what he wants people around him to believe. There shouldn't be anything that Antonio cannot do, won't do, but don't cross him or he'll turn, quickly and savagely, like a cat and . . . and . . . maybe yell loudly. For basically Antonio is a good guy who just wants to get his job done in the most amicable way possible, so that he can get home to his wife and three-year-old child — and so that eventually he can take the two of them and return home to the Azores.

That's Antonio's dream. He got it from his father, who this fall is going to make his come true. For twenty years that old man has worked two jobs, lived simply, given his family just enough, and squirreled the rest away. Now he will return home to the family farm, where he plans to live like a Dom for the remainder of his life.

And Antonio is preparing a similar course. Although he was only twelve when his father finally sent for the rest of the family, thirteen years ago, and although he has been educated and raised to the "good dreams" that comprise America, Antonio sought out a Portuguese girl who shared his aspirations. And like his father they live simply, making do, getting by, and burying every dollar they can do without.

But the "like father, like son" legacy stops with Antonio. His brother Manny has only one desire in life and that is to "boogie" as much as possible. Even as he stands at parade rest against the dividing wall, his palms fixed atop a steel rod, his hips are slightly swaying and his boots are shuffling to the fifties rock that is blasting out of the space-age car-radio contraption Hack wired together one weekend.

Manny is only twenty-one, but has been with the company three years already. Antonio got him the job and he keeps a close, Old World eye on the kid, making certain that when

Manny is on the job, he's doing the job. Tony is unmarried, is between girlfriends, and is investing heavily in a bright red Thunderbird which currently sports every convenience a kid who likes to boogie can squeeze onto and into it. He is also not much bigger or stronger than "Fuck 'Em" William, but is going to work shoulder-to-shoulder with his brother.

And then there is Arthur "Rocko" Robestelli. Rocko stands roughly five feet ten inches tall and weighs out at a fast-rising two hundred and thirty pounds. His chins are commencing to rest on his chest, and he has stopped mustering the effort to shave every day, so that his cheeks are reminiscent of a poorly plucked chicken. Rocko is balding. He chews a toothpick when not smoking, and today is in the clutches of a severe case of laryngitis, which has him growling.

Rocko's favorite expression is "Doesn't anyone around here have a sense of humor?" The answer is "Yes, quite a few do," but that isn't exactly what Rocko is referring to. Behind him against the outside wall of the cutting room are stacks of steel bars on shelves. All the bars are mistakes, future knives that were cut too short. They are spray-painted on the ends and numbered in chalk on top so as to differentiate between the various alloys and tempers that went into producing them. That abundant stock with yellow butts marked 13-0-4 represents over five thousand dollars' worth of miscut knives, one morning's work for Rocko, a quarter of an inch short, each of them. Unfortunately for the company, these also represent the shortest knives Pennington Inc. makes, so that the entire stack is useless except as very expensive scrap.

Foreman Walt Poirier gave him hell. So did plant supervisor Bud Darcy. Bart Pennington was Manufacturing vice-president then, but he never heard about it. Rocko said: "Jesus, doesn't anyone around here have a sense of humor?" When people say: "If there weren't a union around here, there'd be a lot of guys who wouldn't be around either," they are talking, for one, about Rocko Robestelli.

"Okay, men, let's get another one."

This is *the* moment. There is no other point in any other operation in the company to rival it. It is a moment which continues to create as much awe in the hearts and stomachs of the hard-bitten old-timers as it does in those of the newcomers. Even old Carlo Orsini and Jimmy Ouellette will sometimes sneak away from their machines to steal a peek and remember the "good years" when they were the rolling mill crew.

The men stand poised in position, hands and forearms covered in silver asbestos gloves, thick, dark goggles down over their eyes, their bodies tense.

In the dim light, the ancient, battered, dust- and grease- and slag-covered rollers and cast-iron power hammers standing tall, the enormous flywheel of the rolling machine reaching around high toward the blackened ceiling in its ponderous, ceaseless, counterclockwise rotation. The twin forges, side-by-side along the wall, their fires raging, roaring inside, their heat almost unbearable.

Antonio nods.

And the heavy forge door clangs upward. A blast of heat. Faces turn red, turn away. Antonio with tongs, poking and prodding the inferno, chin stuck up, eyes peering down along his nose line, seeking out the sparkling white-red bar. His hands on the long handles come together. He arches his back, breaking the inertia, stepping back. Carefully. A slow dance. The bright bar glides out of the infernal maw and down onto the rod, which, a minute ago, had been Manny's staff, Manny now holding one end, Rocko the other.

"LET'S GO!"

Manny backs up and around to his right with short, quick steps. Rocko follows around with long, sure paces. Antonio backs straight to the hammer. The three set the bar, suddenly deep red, on the anvil. Rocko drops the rod, grabs the tongs, clutches the ends onto the bar.

"LET'S GO!"

Hack trips the hammer. Whbang! Whbang! Whbang! Rapid-fire, deafening. Rocko pulls the bar under the battering hammer. The bar is squashed out under the tremendous pounding, the harder cutting and the softer backing steels being united inseparably. Antonio pulls back, twisting the battered bar to keep it under the hammer, to keep the bar from being thrown off the anvil, to keep from breaking wrists, forearms. Fiery pieces of slag spray helter-skelter against pants, shoes, arms, sides of the face. Back — forth — back.

"LET'S GO!"

Manny again with the rod under the bar, Rocko back on the other end, leading Antonio to the rolling machine, setting the end of the bar between the great rollers. Manny lets go of the rod, Rocko holds on to it, running to the other side, sticking it back under to catch the flattened, elongated bar as it emerges, squeezes out, and begins to drop toward the floor. Hack snatches the bar's end with the tongs, pulling it out, around, following Rocko and Manny toward the straightening hammer.

WHUNK! WHUNK! WHUNK! Banging the ends, sealing them tight. WHUNK! WHUNK! WHUNK! Thumping a warp out.

"LET'S GO!"

Back to the rolling machine, through the top rollers, back through the bottom rollers.

"LET'S GO!"

Back to the straightening hammer. Hold it steady. Eyeball it. Move it up. HOLD IT. WHUNK! Back a little, that small bow. HOLD IT. WHUNK!

"LET'S GO!"

Over to the trolley by the wall. Set it neatly side-by-side with the last one. Rocko places weights on the ends, carefully, to keep them from warping up when the bar cools, trying not to let the weights tip him over on the now dark gray, so recently white-red, recently three-foot-long, now eight-foot-long bar, wary of sizzling an eight-inch stripe across his gut the way he did last year.

"THAT'S IT, MEN!"

Hack goes back to the desk and takes off his gloves and lights up a cigarette. Rocko tucks his gloves under his left arm and lights up a cigarette. Antonio and Manny pick up another short, thick eighty-pound bar off the cold pile and heave it into the forge before they ditch their gloves and light up cigarettes.

Hack checks the tally.

"Twelve down, twenty-one to go. Cheer up. It could be in the middle of the fucking summer."

"Ain't that the fucking truth," agrees "Fuck 'Em" William. Rocko Robestelli spits on the floor.

11

Bruno Baron, THUNKer

★

There might be some debate about this, but the most important person in the back shop might well be Bruno Baron. Some may point to Bud Darcy, the supervisor, or Walt Poirier, the floor foreman. Others might say Guido Orsini of Quality Control or Hod Grady, the shop steward, in the packing room. There is no arguing that each of these men has responsibilities in excess of his fellow workers', who punch in, punch out, and in between may accomplish eighty percent of what is expected of them.

But still, Bruno Baron may be the most important because only he really knows how to THUNK, and without someone knowing how to THUNK accurately and rapidly, the back shop would come to a standstill.

Now Bruno doesn't call what he does THUNKing. He calls it straightening, which is more formal, but less to the point. Not that straightening isn't what he does. It is. Exactly. But the secret to straightening lies in the ability to THUNK, and that calls for an aptitude that is God-given and a skill that is mastered only with time and desire.

And time is something that Bruno has on his side, twenty-two years of it, all spent straightening knives. The man he replaced had performed this essential act for thirty years. To underscore this aspect, over the past fifty of the company's seventy-five years, only two men have handled the straightening assignment — and the rock upon which the company was founded and continues to stand is knives — more accurately, straight knives.

To underscore Bruno's central role further, on its passage from heat treat through the grinding and sharpening processes to the packing room, a knife must pass through Bruno's hands for THUNKing at least three times. It is no accident, therefore, that Bruno Baron's sphere of influence is located smack in the middle of Building 1 where, as to Rome, all oblique paths around machines, materials, tables, lockers, and workers eventually lead.

Bruno is over behind K-6 and is in the process of straightening — that is, THUNKing — a pallet of thirty-six-inch knives. It must be understood that hard and cold and inflexible as a bar of steel may appear, it is, like wood, susceptible to the effects of hot and cold. A one-by-three-inch oak board left out in the sun is going to warp. Similarly, a bar of steel won't warp in the sun, but it will in a five-hundred-degree oven or after a grindstone has been running back and forth over its edge for forty-five minutes. For the most part the warp or warps will not be excessive, most hardly visible to the average eye. Yet a deflection of a mere two or three thousandths of an inch can cause a knife not to fit in place, or to make a deviant cut. As the sign fixed to the I-beam diagonally over Bruno Baron's head reads: RE-MEMBER — THE NEXT INSPECTOR IS THE CUSTOMER.

Bruno takes such admonitions seriously. He sincerely believes that he serves two masters — the company in the form of Frank and Bart, not his immediate superiors, and the anonymous Customer. That is why he feels he is so essential to the system. He sees the material as it passes through heat treat, as it passes through grinding and drilling and shaping and sharpening. He feels he is Quality Control's man on the spot. He is the one man on the floor who touches every single knife. This is a responsibility not to be taken lightly.

Which is why he takes his time THUNKing. The tool he has for the purpose has the prehistoric look of a heron. It also somewhat resembles a large bandsaw or a manual bottle capper. It consists of a steel bed, off the back of which arches a cast-iron neck which swoops up until its peak is dead center over the bed. Attached to the side of the peak is a long lever, much like a water pump handle. When the handle is pulled downward, a piston descends toward the bed until it squares onto the waiting knife. It is at this point that the dextrous art of THUNKing commences.

The knives Bruno is working on have been beveled, but the edges have yet to be ground. This gives him some latitude in handling them. He sets a knife, back edge down, onto the bed, and along its face he lays a straightedge. Bruno can now see the valleys between the knife and the straightedge, can judge the degree of warp. For instance, this knife has a small bow which extends almost the entire length. Logic dictates that the way to get such a bow out is to press down in the middle. This is where Bruno's wealth of experience expresses itself. He is going to defy that logic.

Bruno flips the knife over so that the broad side rests flat on two narrow bars of steel, which elevate it slightly above the bed. He slides the knife to his left so that only the first six inches are dead center. Now he reaches up, grabs the long lever, and slowly, confidently, pulls it down so that the piston is about to touch the knife and — THUNK — a quick tap, firm, not aggressive — and the lever rises upward, the piston retreats, and Bruno slides the knife along another six inches. The THUNKing is repeated, over and over, until the end of the knife is reached.

Bruno now folds the knife back on its edge and reapplies the straightedge. The bow is gone. He picks it up, carries it over to a highly milled steel slab, and lays it down flat. Bruno jabs the edges with a two-mil feeler gauge, rechecking for warps. The gauge slides easily under the first four inches of the lower right-hand corner. Immediately, Bruno tries the upper left-hand corner. Precisely the same four inches are raised. The knife may be flat along its length, but it is twisted diagonally.

He picks up the knife again and lays it this time on the bed of a nearby machine that looks like a drill press. The "drill press" is simply a stationary vertical tube, under which he places one of the raised corners. Between the metal of the knife and the base of the tube he inserts a brass weight. Brass, being soft, will not scar the knife's surface when pressure is placed upon it. Which is what is about to happen. He now grabs a long iron shaft with a narrow U-shaped hook at the end. He fits the hook over the far corner of the knife and, standing at the end of the shaft, he firmly tugs down, releases, tugs down, releases, again letting experience dictate how much pressure should be exerted.

He sets the shaft aside, pulls the brass weight out, hoists the knife to the table, and recommences jabbing with the feeler gauge. Perfect. He lays the knife on an empty dolly and returns for the next knife.

Bruno makes the job look easy. Anyone could learn the rudiments in a short period of time. What distinguishes straightening from just about all the other work is that, first, it is fully manual: at no point is a button pushed or a switch flicked; and second, it requires judgment and skill every time it is performed. Each knife poses a different problem.

There is a story, probably apocryphal, about a small town that had its own electric company. One day, the generators went dead, and for hours the town was without lights. There was no one in the plant who could discover the cause of the failure. In despair, it was recollected that there was an old man still living in the town who had overseen the installation of the generators. He was sent for. He looked about, asked for a hammer, and whacked one of the machines twice. The generators went back to whirring. A week later the town received his bill — for $1002 — itemized as follows: "Each whack, one dollar. Knowing where to whack, one thousand dollars."

Bruno Baron knows where to whack, or in his case, THUNK. He knew that to take the bow out of the knife by pressing in the middle would only make two bows, that he virtually had to roll the bow out as you would a piecrust — or a kinked back. And he knew precisely, not approximately, the amount of thrust to apply to bring the knife into line and not push the bow in the other direction. What's more, he can do it fast and uncomplainingly. It is possible to have one man be the focal point through which all the company's knives must pass and still keep up with production schedules and maintain satisfied customers — as long as that one man is Bruno Baron.

That is why Bruno may be the most important person in the back shop. He is irreplaceable. Three to five men would be needed to do his work at his pace and accuracy. Yet there is no one in the company whose job is less translatable outside the confines of Pennington Inc. Where, except for another knife manufacturer, would there be any call for a man with twenty-two years' experience in THUNKing knives? If the company were to fold and Bruno were on the street, he would be less desirable than the nineteen-year-old kid on K-8 with two years' experience setting knives on a movable bed, setting a dial, pushing a button, then spending the next half hour, arms crossed on an already spreading gut, toe-tapping to the latest offering of AC/DC, a kid who pumped gas at Arnie's Sunoco around the corner for his first job out of high school, who still lives with his parents and tosses his entire week's paycheck ($7.65 per hour) into a black Camaro.

But, according to Bruno, Bruno Baron on the street is as unlikely as Frank, Harold, or Bart Pennington on the street. To make that a reality the company would have to cease to exist, and it never will. Things may be looking slow right now, but you have to have the right perspective. Sure, there have been layoffs and a week's shutdown, but look at the numbers. There are as many people working for the company now as there ever were. All those people that were laid off, they'd only been added on for a couple or three years, so that now things are back to where they used to be all along. And maybe there aren't as many knives going out the door as a year ago. That's all right. There are still more going out than five years ago.

This is how you gotta figure it, says Bruno: back before the last major recession in the mid-seventies, the company had a lot more competition. Then a lot of those guys, being as they were smaller and couldn't hack it, went under, and Pennington Inc. picked up their business. Which was about when the third shift went on. So the same thing's happening now. The small guys will turn turtle, the big guys will snatch up the trade, and everything will be the way it used to be. And Bruno will go on THUNKing all day, go home to the wife, have a little supper, watch some TV, and hit the rack by eight-thirty — except on Wednesdays, which is payday for him and the Mrs., who assembles computers at Eliot Corp. On Wednesdays, they go to the mall after supper.

12

The Boys of the Packing Room

★

The Pennington Golf Team has long been a source of division in the back shop. Somehow in the course of its evolution, it has come to represent the elite. If you are on the Pennington Golf Team, particularly if you sport the silky gold warm-up jacket with the Pennington Golf Team monogram over the left breast and your name stitched in blue on the left shoulder, you can walk tall, even brazenly, about the shop; you can swing your hips a little and whack the others on the ass, even give a little grab and make the kind of obscene remark which, elsewhere, would probably get you a mouthful of busted teeth from someone much like yourself.

It is hard to pinpoint the source of the golf team's eminence, for, if the truth be told, there is very little selection involved. Those people who make the team are those who sign up for it in the spring. And those people who wear the official jackets are those willing to put up the money. What's more, the word *team* is a misnomer, since there are no outside contests, just friendly, beer-swilling, eighteen-hole hackfests in which the willingness to bend an elbow is as highly valued as the ability to chip out of the bunker.

Perhaps it is because golf alone remains the one thing everyone in the company, front office as well as back shop, can do together. Once there were company softball and bowling teams. There is a trophy case near the men's room in Building 1, on the other side of the wall from the time clock, with bowling and softball trophies that date back to the late 1950s. There are "remember when" stories, like the time Frank Pennington was down in Philadelphia at a meeting and he chartered a plane to fly back for a special challenge match, returning to Philadelphia immediately afterward. That was a long time ago. Only the old men recall it. They also remember that Harold used to be a good bowler, too. It was the only time they ever saw him, even then.

Bowling died when the Southside lanes up at the corner of the green folded. And softball died when the old men refused to play with the younger guys, who themselves refused to play unless they could carry their beer onto the field with them. As old Jimmy Ouellette recollects: "When I and Pauly was growing up, we played ball anywhere we could, any time we could squeeze it in between school and jobs. We lived baseball. Now you got a bunch of kids that don't know how to throw, not mentioning hitting the cutoff man. You try to teach 'em, what do they care? Here comes a ball to my second baseman, an easy chance, and what's he doing? The guy's got a brew in his hand and he's chugging the whole thing while there goes the ball — boombiddy, boombiddy — by him. I seen that, I quit . . . and that's why Pennington Inc. ain't got no more softball."

Only golf has survived, to come to the fore every Thursday at three o'clock in the afternoon, starting in May, ending in late August with a blowout beer blast, which has been the ruination of even Bart a few times.

You will notice that golf starts at three o'clock, when the team gathers around the time clock, not at three-thirty, when everyone else punches out. This is the major bone of contention. The nongolfers could probably accept the early quitting time, if they were not reminded of it by the golfers, who persist in mocking their less fortunate union brothers.

Last Thursday the Pennington Golf Team jibed too far, and the next day Hack Harden complained. First he went to his foreman, Walt Poirier, who told him there was nothing he would do, that for years the Golf Team had left early, that this practice had the tacit approval of the authorities, and Hack would be advised to stuff his complaint. Walt, of course, is a jacket-wearing member of the golf team.

Hack contemplated complaining to Building 1 supervisor Bud Darcy but stopped with the contemplation. Bud Darcy was the head of the Pennington golf program. So, being a dues-paying member in good standing of Union Local 1705 of the International Brotherhood of Allied Machinists, Hack filed a complaint with the two shop stewards of Building 1 — Hod Grady and Steve Corbett. Hod spoke for Steve and himself when he explained to Hack what could be done with the complaint. He was even wearing his gold jacket at the time.

Hack swore then that he would never trust the fucking union again.

As for Hod and Steve, they both went back to work in the packing room.

You can enter the packing room through doors by the rolling mill, between K-9 and K-11, or from the loading bay. It is a low-ceilinged, four-square concrete-block room, which, in contrast with most other work spaces in the building, is well lit and clean. It and the loading dock comprise the newest additions to the plant.

The Professor is sitting in the far corner of the packing room, hunched over his desk with his chin on the heel of one hand, a pencil in the other. He appears to be completing some paperwork, which he has set out in front of him. The drawer under the desk top is pulled out and there is a paperback in there, open. The Professor is taking a chapter break.

The other three men in the packing room are, right to left: Hod Grady over at the center table packing long knives; Steve Corbett at the bench in the middle of the room packing chipper knives; and Harve Grenier by the window honing long knives. There is one radio on the window sill by Harve — WRDY — playing oldies but goodies, at the moment blasting "Corina, Corina" by Clyde McFatter.

Hod has been with the company thirteen years and has a brother in Quality Control with twenty years behind him. Both Hod and his brother have served as shop stewards. The brother is now part of management. Hod carries on for both of them. Steve has ten years with the company and has a wife in Finance with eight. Harve has six years and his brother in the warehouse five. Their father had thirty-one before he retired five years ago. Harve began on June 7, 1979. He remembers the date exactly because it was the Monday after his high school graduation. And that day he remembers proudly because, of his sixty-five siblings and cousins, he is the only one with a high school diploma.

The packing room marks the final step before the knives reach the loading platform and head for the customer. It is here that imperfections have to be discovered and, if possible, corrected. It is also here that cutting edges are given their final honing. This is Harve's job.

In a way, this is one of the more dangerous jobs on the floor, for by this point the knives are only a few strokes away from ready. They are already sharp enough to shave with. And some of them weigh up to seventy pounds, and are an unwieldy four to five feet long. If one were to drop, edge first, it would neatly slice into, even through, a foot, a shank, or a forearm.

Harve's task is to hone the edge to a near-microscopic line, free of any burrs that could mar a cut. The tool he uses resembles a medium-size block plane fixed to roller skates, the rollers of which are set close together and angled to form a V. The V fits over the beveled edge of the knife, and the honing occurs as Harve runs the rollers over the cutting surface, back and forth, smoothly, evenly, his elbows out like wings so that his forearms do not come near the edge, his feet shuffling forward in a two-step, never crossing, because doing that might cause him to lose his balance and fall on the knife.

On the window ledge is a pile of scrap paper that has been ripped in roughly three-by-five-inch rectangles. When he thinks he has the edge right, Harve takes a piece of the paper, bends it between his thumb and the first two fingers of his right hand, giving it a slight belly, like a half cone, to stiffen it. Then, with a series of deft sweeps of his wrist, he flicks the paper along the edge of the knife, causing the paper to be sliced up in curves, leaving it looking like a grass hula skirt. If there is any imperfection on the cutting edge, it will catch the paper. The hitch in the flow of the paper will be almost imperceptible, but Harve's trained fingers are sensitive to any irregularities. He does not have any idea how many thousands of knives, how many miles of knife, he has swept paper over. He takes pride in saying that all *his* knives are flawless. He sincerely believes that he has developed a special skill that he is certain he could market if the company were to close up shop tomorrow.

Unfortunately, the Professor possesses the same skill along with greater seniority. Next week, Harve goes out to the yard to drive the forklift. When business gets better, he says, he'll be back.

Hod's job is to pack the knives Harve has honed. One at a time he lifts a finished knife off the wagon Harve is filling and lays it flat upon a long, highly machined, well-dusted steel slab much like the one Bruno Baron uses in his THUNKing process. He searches around for his .002 feeler gauge, which he then jabs along the edge between the knife and the slab. If he finds any warp, he takes up the knife and sets it on another wagon. When there are enough rejects to justify a trip — and that number varies with Hod's mood or energy level — he'll mosey the wagon out to Bruno Baron for restraightening.

The passable knives he cautiously picks up and carries to the bench by the window overlooking the yard. There he stencils on the company's "Wolverine Line" stamp, then brushes the entire knife surface with oil to inhibit rusting. Gingerly he sets the knife into a mahogany case (specially made by the company's wood shop), in which it is bolted fast. The lid is screwed down, and the sealed case set aside for shipping. The entire process takes plus or minus ten minutes.

The order calls for forty of these knives to be packed and sent out to Harkness & Bolt, Inc., of Windsor Locks, Connecticut. As "lead man" in the packing room, Hod is responsible for scheduling. The way he figures it at the moment, there is no way he and Harve can complete the full forty without breaking hump. Now there aren't a whole lot of orders coming up, so rather than busting hump today and making work tomorrow, why not just do twenty today and have work for tomorrow? Consequently, Hod has shifted himself down into second gear, stretches each packing job out to fifteen minutes, has offered to fetch the coffee from the canteen, has sought out a couple of guys in grinding whom Hanrahan has been trying to reassign and who have filed a grievance, and has double-checked Steve's work three or four times, just for something to do.

Steve's a good shit. He and Hod, they understand each other; at least Steve understands what Hod says and agrees with him. This is the kind of thing that Hod likes to opine, and which Steve finds simpático: "I've always said that there's only one way to handle prisoners. You put 'em on an island and you hook 'em good on heroin. When they fuck up, you take away their heroin and give the bastards a good case of the jitters."

As an example of how closely attuned their minds are, here is one of Steve's opinions: "Same thing with welfare. You put 'em in a project, fence the sucker off, give 'em something to cook on and wash with — no money — and see how quick they get outa there."

Steve was a high school football player. He pumped a lot of iron back then, which gave him arms the size of the average thigh, big enough to enforce his opinions. He took the state police exams and says he did "real well," only, he adds, the "staties" said he was too heavy. "It was the fuckin' Puerto Ricans that did me outa that," he swears. Understandably he is not too fond of Puerto Ricans or blacks, who are one and the same, and he can barely stand going through heat treat because of Antonio Silva, who is Portuguese.

Steve still dreams of what it might have been to be a state trooper, but he is satisfied packing knives and being a shop steward. That gives him a chance to put it to the bosses, which is what he is planning when contract negotiations start up next month.

Hod is pretty satisfied with himself. He's got a good job, he's got security (you can't bump a shop steward, especially one on the Pennington Golf Team). His old lady's got a good job. And the bosses dislike him, which is just where he wants them. Hod can't wait for the union contract negotiations to start up either.

Harve could be happier. His wife left him a month ago and he's living in a one-room apartment and washing his own clothes. It's a lousy life, but thank God for the Ward 8 Club, where he gets to tend bar some. And he's making decent money, even with having to go back to the yard.

And the Professor? Well, maybe things will get good again and he can go back to nights and a little peace of mind. Still, things could be worse, like he could be digging graves again.

"We'll do that bunch tomorrow," Hod yells over the janglings of Bo Diddley.

"Good with me," Harve yells back.

"What the hell!" Steve sighs, laughing.

The Professor goes over and sits down at his desk and pulls out the drawer. And takes the mark out of his book. There's still half an hour till quitting time.

"Look," Hod says aloud to anyone, "I was reading in the Classifieds about this set of irons. . . ."

13

Pauly

★

"**W**hat do you call three niggers in a dark alley? . . . Sir,
Sir, Sir."

Pauly Ouellette chirrups from behind the steering wheel of
the Pennington Inc. delivery van, delighting in his joke, tickled
that no one had robbed him of the joy of delivering the punch
line.

Who is Pauly Ouellette? Well, first, he is the slightly
younger, six-inch-shorter brother of old Jimmy Ouellette of the
NC Room, which makes him third in company seniority behind Jimmy and Carlo Orsini in the back shop and fourth over-
all when Frank Pennington is included. Pauly has been on the
Pennington payroll since April 23, 1941.

Second, he is the company scrap man, which is the more
formal name for the company gofer. In the public sector Pauly's
position would be the rough equivalent of a lifetime-tenured
assistant clerk of courts for the Third District.

Third, Pauly is a father, husband, Catholic, Elk, taxpayer,
Democrat, and sharpshooter, the order of which changes with
the wind or the morning news.

Fourth, he is the company gossip, being situated by nature
and profession near more ears and mouths than almost anyone
else in the company. Pauly is never short of a ready explanation
for anything that may have happened around the shop or in the
front office. Accuracy is not his forte, however.

Pauly doesn't live more than ten long minutes from the back
gate of the employees' parking lot. He lives in a small yellow

house he has called home for most of the forty-two years he has been employed by the company. Every day without fail he has made the crosstown trip, never late except February 21, 1948, when there was a blizzard. He'd had to walk and he arrived at nine o'clock, only to discover everyone else had been sent home. He remembers that date as though it were an indelible blot on an otherwise impeccable record.

He is a very small man and he drives a small car, which, due to his early morning arrival, he is able to park near the gate, making his walk across the yard up to his locker in the far corner of the machine shop the shortest and most direct route traceable. His locker is tucked out of sight in the far right-hand corner between some storage shelves and the chain link fence that separates the supply room from the rest of the shop. He calls this area "my shop," and, if you didn't know any better, you would swear it was the cell of a man doing five to ten for something as unimpressive as mail fraud or misuse of the phone system. There is a little table with a coffeepot, a jar of instant coffee, some Cremora, and a plastic dish of sugar envelopes. A couple of mugs hang nearby. There is a small wall mirror surrounded by utterly undisturbing pictures of gracious ladies, circa 1944, all on the verge of rendering themselves immodest. "If my wife saw them, she wouldn't mind," Pauly assures himself.

It is in his "shop," away from the other men, that Pauly prepares himself for the duties daily pressed upon him. It is also to his "shop" that he repairs at noon for R&R and, at the end of the workday, for regrooming and a deep breath of relief.

It must be understood that in Pauly's world there are official and unofficial duties, and that only he knows the difference. As far as everyone else is concerned, it's:

"Hey, Pauly, will you get me a couple of packs of Winstons?"

"Hey, Pauly, here's a couple bucks, you want to buy me some lottery tickets?"

Naturally, you would assume these to be the unofficial duties, and you would be right. The official duty that provides the vehicle for these others is the fetching of the company's morning mail from the central post office downtown.

Deadlines in Pauly's line of work are flexible. He does have to punch in and out like everyone else in the back shop, an act of some aggravation to him. Not that he thinks of himself as superior to the others. Rather, it is an act of such gravity that he is actually afraid he will fail to perform it on time and thus will receive yet another black mark beside his name to go with the blizzard of '48.

That constriction aside, he is free to parcel out his workload as he sees fit. Oh, perhaps he ought to have the morning mail back to be sorted by midmorning, but ten o'clock is as defensible as nine-thirty. Which allows for a coffee and muffin at Uncle Ed's Donut Shop on Lafayette Street, where he can squeeze a peep at the *National Inquirer* and maybe run into a couple of guys from the Elks. But before that, there is a stop at Murray's Hardware for some stain the maintenance foreman needs for a bookcase in Bart's office, and there is no sense anyway of getting back too early because, well, you know, you don't want anyone to get the wrong idea, like maybe they could expect the mail sooner. So after Uncle Ed's it's over to the Suffolk Bank and Trust on High Street to deposit his paycheck and take out some money for Fritzie in Production and deposit a check for Sue in Sales, and on the way out grab a handful of complimentary TV guides to leave in the mailroom for anyone who wants one.

The Suffolk Bank and Trust stop borders on legitimate because the post office is only across the street and Pauly can use their respective parking lots interchangeably. At the post office the Pennington drawer is bursting. It takes some time to sort the letters from the magazines from the *Wall Street Journals* and to set each class in its proper place in the unwieldy Pennington pouches, turning each bunch upside down so that

118

when Pat opens the pouches onto the table in the mailroom, everything will slide out name up. Very important. The finickiness of this exercise is relieved by the proximity of the Sanders Bros.' gofer with the long black hair and the jeans, who is sorting her mail across the counter. "The Mrs. would understand," Pauly mumbles.

And it's back to the rat race, back to the company van, lugging the two pouches like a Pony Express rider . . . and out of the van again to run across the street to Dolph's Tobacco Store for Melissa of Finance's cigarettes and Johnny's lottery tickets and, while there anyway, another dollar's worth of chances for the heck of it, for himself, then back to the van and a relaxed ride back to the company.

It is not such a bad life. The fact is, it's pretty good, as long as you play by the rules. And playing by the rules is something Pauly knows all about. Here, for instance, are some of Pauly's rules, which to him have the power of Commandments:

"When the boss tells me: 'Pick that up,' I picks it up. When the boss says: 'Go over there,' I go over there. I wouldn't if I didn't want to, but I don't mind."

Another rule: "When the boss tells me: 'Pauly, don't take no chances,' I don't take no chances."

Which is why he carries a homemade nightstick that is nearly a third his size in the van with him, right in the well between the two front bucket seats. No Puerto Rican or nigger will get the better of Pauly Ouellette — that is, if said Puerto Rican or nigger can get through all the locked doors and rolled-up windows. And when Pauly has to go into the city or to the airport on a night errand, he says he is careful to have one of his pistols with him.

And, according to Pauly, he can use those pistols. It has been some time since he went down to the YMCA range and took target practice, but once upon a time, he was good for a steady ninety-eight, ninety-nine out of hundred, anytime — and he says he can still be counted on for ninety-six right now, stone cold. Guns! He has an arsenal in the basement of his little house. No, he's never shot at anyone, not even in "the war."

That was when he was considerably younger. His knees have become a little more susceptible to terror since, and being around the front office even makes him a little nervous. The front office is where the Bosses walk around in shirtsleeves and crack jokes and laugh and make decisions and tell Pauly what to do. It is also, in a way, where the enemy resides . . . no, not exactly *the* enemy because just about everyone at the company is an enemy of sorts, but . . . the other side. Pauly doesn't want anyone in the back shop to think he might be a brown-noser, an ass-kisser. So he tries to get in, deliver the pouches, cigarettes, lottery tickets, and get out posthaste, while still hanging around a bit to see if there might be some news that might be useful later on.

For being useful, being available, is Pauly's stock in trade. When a part has to be delivered to Cedarsville, Pauly gets the call. When Frank needs a ride to the airport for one of his frequent trips abroad, Pauly is the chauffeur. When the Elks need someone to serve supper at the regular Thursday night potluck affair, there is Pauly. And Pauly is always "there" because, first of all, at Pennington Inc., that is where he is paid to be, and, second, he has designed his life so that he is rarely very far from where he has always been.

As has already been related, Pauly gets up in the morning in plenty of time to be early for work, which is at seven A.M. He is never late. He performs his duties regularly five days a week. (It should be noted that his wife follows much the same routine. She works on an assembly line at Tabor Industries, a large employer of Pennington Inc. wives.) He returns home promptly after punching out at three-thirty P.M., showers, has an early supper, watches some television, and goes to bed at nine P.M.

On Saturdays he eases up a bit, working instead around the house until noon, at which time his daughter comes over for an afternoon of crocheting with her mother. Pauly then takes off for the Elks Hall, where he showers, shaves, then slides up to the bar for his one beer of the week. He nurses this beer along until three o'clock, when he wends his way home in time to take the wife to four o'clock Mass. They attend Mass on Saturday afternoons rather than the more customary Sunday mornings in order to allow her to sleep late and him to sneak off for a couple of strings at the Towne Lyne Alleys. The remainder of Sunday is spent around the house, fixing things. The current project is the front steps. By eight-thirty P.M., Pauly is ready to go to bed. Vacations are distinguished from work weeks by the cancellation of the early morning trip crosstown to Pennington Inc. and the turning of the little car toward Uncle Ed's Donut Shop.

That is Pauly Ouellette's life to date, a two-lane street that leads from home to Pennington Inc. and back with some occasional side trips to the Elks, Mass, the bowling alley, or Uncle Ed's. It lacks the room even for his older brother, Jimmy, who "never returns anything when he comes to borrow something." It cannot even tolerate "Fuck 'Em" William Baxter, who last week inadvertently took Pauly's seat at the Thursday night potluck supper and who has been the focus of Pauly's silent treatment since.

Pauly's life is included here because he deserves as much recognition for services rendered to Pennington Inc. as do the Professor, Bruno Baron, Hod Grady, maybe even Don Schmidt and Willis Farnsworth. He may not know how to THUNK and he may be as reluctant before the rolling mill as his nemesis "Fuck 'Em" William. He may not have the skills of Henry Grandmaison or the encouraging nature of Jake Henchard. And maybe what he does could be accomplished by anyone with a Class 2 license and the need of a job.

And maybe not. Pauly Ouellette has performed his ancillary services, most of which have no effect on the "bottom line," for forty-one years, day after day, with a loyalty beyond doubt or question, through good times and bad. When Pauly retires, maybe the front office will recognize his lengthy tenure with a supper for two at Fenwicks or with a watch like the one old Carlo Orsini longs for. Maybe he'll just be the momentary center of attention between punch-out and lunch one Friday noon in the not-too-distant future. It is all incidental. The gifts have already been exchanged. Pennington Inc. has given Pauly something to do all his life, and Pauly has responded by giving his life to the company.

14
Hanrahan Speaks, the Boys Listen

★

There is only one thing worse than knowing what the bad news is, and that is not knowing. Which is the state the back shop generally finds itself in. The grapevine can sketch broad outlines of what news might be pending, but its accuracy is often skewed by the degree to which the bearer deems himself to be in the know. The closer to the "facts" the bearer thinks he is, the farther removed from the "truth" he seems to be. Take Bruno Baron, the THUNKer: "With all the people [company president] Schmidt knows in the business, all he has to do when times get bad is get on the phone and say, we've got some knives, you must need some."

Bruno is certain this is the way the front office operates because he feels he stands very close with the powers that be, particularly with the Penningtons. He insists, "When I don't like something, when I think something is wrong, I don't waste time going to [supervisor] Darcy. I go right to Frank or Bart. I'm not afraid of walking right into the office and telling either one what's going on and maybe what he should do about it."

Although no one has ever witnessed this, it might be true, or at least true he did it once. It is true that the other day Frank was showing some Japanese visitors through the plant and happened to pass by the THUNKing area. Bruno nearly rolled over on his back and barked when the chairman of the board merely nodded.

It is also probable that Bruno would be thunderstruck to learn that Don Schmidt not only has few contacts within the industry, but that he instead calls in his VPs to see if they have any chits outstanding.

All of which is to show that in the best of times the back shop is like a caboose. It has no real idea where the front office is taking it, and as times grow worse, it follows credulously. Even as company doctor H. Edwin Blatchford was telling the board of trustees that unless something was done to shape up the company, the next act could be the locking of the gates, the men in the back shop were blithely assuring one another that the worst was over. That's what they'd heard.

So when it was learned that Manufacturing's Gerry Hanrahan was in Bud Darcy's office along with the foremen and the shop stewards, a trembling set in. Instead of the usual standing around by their machines and staring at the sun-driven fairies playing among the girders or at their oil-spattered boots, the men tended to chat with each other, not always about the meeting that they knew was going on behind the wall, but about "things." A lot of "whatever happened to?" — that sort of nervous, casual curiosity — about someone who had been bumped out during the recent layoffs. Sometimes they'd start a conversation like that and it would peter out after a "don't know," and they'd stand there in silence.

And the meeting went on and on. It had started at eight that morning and it was ten, then ten-thirty. Even Bruno Baron grew itchy and wandered over to heat treat and stood around while everybody watched Antonio snack from a bowl of boiled potatoes, onions, beans, carrots, and . . . "No shit! Horse meat?! Only you black bastards would eat that shit." To which Antonio answered: "Try some, you ball-less Canuck," and, grinning, held a forkful out to Bruno, who was on the edge of retching anyway. And Antonio forked the whole bite into his mouth, wiped the corners with his sleeve, and slowly masticated, leering at everyone.

At eleven, Hod Grady and Steve Corbett, the Building 1

shop stewards, appeared on the floor. They swaggered a bit, for they were the emissaries, the ones with the news. This was their opportunity for center stage and they both, especially Hod, were determined to milk out every drop.

"Hanrahan's going to meet with everyone next week."

That was their teaser, but it wasn't what the men wanted to hear. Was the company shutting down? Were there going to be any more layoffs? Were their jobs on the line? What was happening?

"Ask Hanrahan next week. He says he wants to get to know you; he wants you to know him. He says he wants you to ask anything that's on your mind. Let it all hang out, he says."

That was good enough for some of the men. If Hanrahan was going to see them next week, then they'd have to be there to be seen, which meant there was work, so the hell with it. It wasn't enough for others. Hack Harden wanted to know: "Layoff or not?" — "Ask Hanrahan." — "Hey!" So Hod wisely let slip that the union had been assured there would be no more layoffs, no shutdowns this month, probably none next month, maybe a short shutdown before the summer shutdown in late July for vacation. Maybe.

That was all anyone wanted to know. With the release of that information Hod and Steve had surrendered their hostages. They wandered among the machines, waiting to be asked what else went on in that three-hour meeting with all the important people, among whom were counted Hod and Steve. But no one cared. It was the same old story with the happy ending. When push came to shove, the Penningtons took care of their people. Just get up in the morning and get to work on time and you could stay with Pennington Inc. until the Final Friday.

Their sudden diffidence did not mean the men weren't curious to meet Hanrahan. Who was this guy anyway? He'd been there for four months and most of the men had hardly laid eyes on the guy, much less talked to him. They all knew Bart, of course. Bart had never called them together. He'd come out and bullshit with them on the line. You couldn't talk with Frank. No one had really ever known Harold, but Bart was people, even if he was an owner and a millionaire (which everyone knew for a certainty, even if they were not twenty-five percent accurate). The loss of Bart and the arrival of Hanrahan had left a void. That was what Hanrahan was: a void, a faceless, almost bodiless presence that had somehow been responsible for the loss of large numbers of their body and that they instinctively sensed they ought to beware of. From what they could gather, whoever this Hanrahan was, he wasn't on their side. So, when the word came down the following Wednesday: "The man's seeing you guys today," the men were ready for a little seeing of their own.

Hanrahan is receiving in the smaller of the two conference rooms in PRC. To get there the men have to go through the sliding metal door that separates the back shop from the front office, down the long corridor by Production, hard right at Hanrahan's and Harold Pennington's offices, hard left at Ida Bright's personnel office, on by the committee room, by the "honor roll," hard right by Finance, and hard left out the main doors in front of receptionist Gladys Hale.

This is foreign country. Most of the men who have even been through the sliding door had stopped at Personnel. A few have made it to Bart's office on an errand. Some have had to work out insurance problems with Finance. Most of the men are uncomfortable and tend to band together, talking brazenly, their eyes wide open, like children in a museum. They bound down the stairs, through the glass doors, out to Beauchamp Street, and across to PRC like children released for recess.

The smaller conference room is scaled down to essentials. It was designed for groups determined to stick to particular company business. No deals are swung in the smaller conference room. It is lighter than the executive room next door, with windows on two sides. There is a chalkboard on the inner wall and a desk and chair in front of it. There is even a lectern to the right of the desk.

To the left of the blackboard are four black-and-white photographs. Two show a lineup of 1958 retirees. One is woodshop foreman John Genest's father, another is old Carlo Orsini's. Carlo himself is in the room, along with his two sons, Guido of Quality Control and Mickey of the welding shop. When that picture was taken, Carlo had already put in twenty-three of his current forty-seven years. The elder Orsini had spent thirty-five years with the company. Carlo looks as though he could step into the photograph, his father out, and no one would know the difference. And both Guido and Mickey look like *their* father.

There is another photograph, probably taken in the mid-twenties, when the company was beginning its major expansion. It is a group picture of the entire back shop then. A hard-looking crew. One company tale has it that the founder, Arthur M., would stand at the local train station and snag French-Canadian immigrants as they arrived from the provinces looking for work. He allegedly treated them as conscriptees and paid them accordingly. That is what is said, and the men in the picture do not dispute it, especially the young boys, who appear as tired as their elders.

On the far wall are four photographs from the seventy-fifth anniversary. One of them shows Carlo Orsini, the company's longest-tenured employee, presenting a plaque to the chairman of the board, Frank Pennington, the eldest active owner. Both are smiling warmly.

Two rows of metal folding chairs have been set up in a squared-off U facing the desk, giving a further impression of school, the only ingredients missing being paper and pencils. And when Hanrahan walks in, the light burble of chatter dissolves into anticipatory silence.

Hanrahan assumes his seat at the desk, crosses his arms in front of him, and slowly surveys the men before him, starting left to right, a reserved yet sympathetic smile on his face. He has put on weight in the months he has been on the job.

"Good morning," he starts, "I'm glad you could make it." He smiles. The men grin, their eyes riveted on him.

"There've been a lot of rumors, a lot of speculation concerning what's going on with the company, and I thought that it would be a good thing to sit down with you and let you know as much as I can about what is happening.

"The way I see it, our level of business is tied very closely to the economy, which all of you are aware isn't very good at the moment. According to our industrial utilization and capacity figures, we are working at only seventy-one percent of capacity — which is probably of no surprise to you on the floor — and this is because we are down forty percent on our orders.

"I'll be honest with you; this is the worst quarter for us in the past five years, and my personal prediction is that it's going to be slow right through the summer. It won't be until fall that we will see any improvement, if there is any."

There is a monotone to his delivery, not quite like a recording, but close. Hanrahan's talent lies in the uncovering of numbers and revealing the story they tell. This can be effective in an argument with Sales or Finance; it can be tedious for people used to dealing in short sentences. Already there is some looking out the window, some blank expressions that state baldly: "I could've told you this was going to be a big, fucking waste of time. These guys don't never tell you nothing." The shop stewards, Hod and Steve, are paying attention, however. They are well aware that the union contract talks are about to begin, and they are already sensing a "poor mouth" proposal from Hanrahan.

But Hanrahan is not as much one of "these guys" as the men assume. Unlike Bart, Harold, or Frank, unlike Searles, Wilton, Schmidt, and Farnsworth, Hanrahan is the son of a high ironworker. His education has been in the trades, not the liberal arts. He has lived in the midst of unions and ward bosses, and even if it has been a long time since he wore a blue collar, the men sense he had, that at one point he was a "brother," and that maybe he was giving out some straight shit.

"The company lives off the money it is able to put aside, and that has not been very much in the past years. The trouble is, we cannot dominate a market. There is true competition we face. We need new equipment, new kinds of knives. We've had no substantial profits while incurring some substantial losses. What we need is a better mix of products. To do that we must do substantially better in planning, and we have a long way to go to improve that. . . . Meanwhile, we must make maximum use of inventory, although what we use may not be the ideal material for the job 'cause it's the costs that are hurting us, and one of our bigger costs is inventory.

"We have a very large facility for the size of our operation. This means very large fixed costs. It would be nice if we could sell off part of this facility, but that's not feasible.

"Now I'm pretty confident we will survive. I don't expect to see any more layoffs, but we may have further shutdowns. We're in a very slow and difficult spring and summer, but the annual cycle means that come November, December, there ought to be an influx, and from the looks of things we'll have some orders in winter.

"That's about all I can tell you from what I know. I'm sure you've got some questions for me. I'll do my best to answer them, so why don't you go ahead."

There is a heavy-breathing silence. The men were just beginning to get settled on Hanrahan's bus when suddenly the "everybody off" call went out. They are panicked. They'd liked what Hanrahan had said; that is, they'd liked the way he'd said it. It was honest-like and no bullshit. And while he hadn't said anything they didn't think they already knew, he was the big honcho saying it right out to them. They appreciated that.

But, Jesus, now they have to speak! It is one thing to tell everybody about how you tell the bosses this and that and how you don't take nothing from you don't care who. It is another thing to open your mouth in public, all by your lonesome, and tell the boss what's on your mind, especially a boss you've never talked to before, hardly ever seen before, who comes into the place and before you even know his name has buried a whole bunch of your union brothers and looks as though he could bury you if he had to.

"What are you goin' to do about summer hours? There was a time there we'd start at six so's we could get out at two and do something?"

All eyes travel over to the far corner to the mustachioed kid who might have stepped out of the group picture on the wall. He is leaning back in his chair and gives a little flick of his head, acknowledging the appreciation of his peers for breaking the silence.

Hanrahan's answer is perfectly genial and short: "I'm inclined to leave the hours the way they are." There is no explanation. There is no argument. There is nothing lost in trying.

Again fidgety silence.

"What are you going to do about improving the rolling mill?"

There is a sudden focusing of all eyes on Bruno Baron. There is also a wave of tension. Even Hanrahan feels it. Someone has dared to ask a serious and potentially embarrassing question right in front of all the people who have to be involved in the answer.

"We're going to make every effort to keep all work in the shop," Hanrahan answers. "We're currently trying to get contract work to defray expenses. Herman Polan is in charge of that and he's looking at some government contracts."

"That's not what I'm talking about," Bruno shoots back. "I'm talking about the ten, fifteen percent waste on most of the knives coming outa the rolling mill. Dicky here will tell you — ain't it right — everytime you trim up a knife, you gotta cut off a foot, foot 'n' a half, 'cause the weld didn't take? Which is a lot of waste you can't use. My feeling is, there's too much turnover in that department, too many people that don't know what's what."

"There's a lot of excuses, that's what," growls old Carlo Orsini, who had appeared to be sleeping throughout the proceedings, but has risen from the dead to give a boost to the old guard.

"Carlo, how long you been off the rolling mill?" asks foreman Walt Poirier.

"'s been four years now," Carlo answers, settling back in his folding chair, arms crossed, left leg over right knee, something close to a smirk on his face.

"That's when it started, when Carlo left," Walt offers Hanrahan.

"It puzzles me why a problem has sat around so long and not been redressed," Hanrahan muses. "Then again, there might not have been the driving force in the past there is today."

Not only has Hanrahan put on weight over the past four months, he has exchanged kid gloves for twelve ouncers and is throwing some timely and thoughtful punches at some heavyweight targets, for who else could he have meant by "driving force" but Schmidt and the Penningtons (lack of) and himself (presence of).

But even Hanrahan recognizes the enormity of his allusion and quickly moves to ameliorate. "I'm daily impressed by how much this company means to the owners. I'm impressed that they have not taken very much out of it. They could have, and no one would have held it against them, but they are not so interested in return on investment. It's the business and the people that mean the most to them, and that is one of the strongest assets we have.

"Irregardless, we still have a lot of work to do," he adds.

"What about the machinery that's always breaking down? What about some preventive maintenance?" Hod Grady asks from "managers' corner" where sit Building 1 supervisor Bud Darcy and all the foremen, as well as the shop stewards.

"I know what you are asking," Hanrahan answers. "There are differences in philosophies. You're wondering: if there is so little work, why not shut a machine down and overhaul it? Why wait until it breaks down when you need it? The question is: where the heck do I get the money to pay for fixing it? It may not make much sense, but the machine has to be working to make the money to pay for its repairs if it stops working. That's where the company is right now."

"Hey, Mr. Hanrahan, what about doing something about the ventilation windows? In the morning it's smoky as a bastard in there." This is from the same kid who wondered about the summer hours.

Hanrahan smiles. It is almost as though the kid were a plant, put there to ask answerable questions.

"Jack, will you handle that? See what can be done?" Hanrahan asks, turning toward the maintenance foreman, Jack Devoe. He nods and Hanrahan stands up.

"Again I want to thank all of you for coming and I want you to know, any questions, you make sure you bring them to me."

He smiles benevolently and walks out the door.

It is reasonable to assume that the front office in the person of Gerry Hanrahan did not lose anything from its gesture to the back shop. On the other hand, it probably didn't win much either. At best the illusion of equality was perpetuated among those for whom that illusion is necessary, that illusion that everybody is in the battle together. And while the roles may differ, obliging some to give, others to receive orders, still the effort is shared. Bruno has to believe he can tell Bart where the bear shits in the woods. Gerry Hanrahan has to believe he can be candid with the men.

The fact is, everybody hears what he wants to hear, and most of that is what each has previously composed. Hanrahan heard nothing new from the men. He didn't expect he would, not in a group like that, not with Darcy, Poirier, and the rest listening. Who was going to have the nerve to say: "One of the problems you've got back there is that you've got a bunch of bosses who don't know as much about the machines as us that work on 'em." Or, in the words of planer Rolly Camille: "What's this guy going to tell me when what I know about this job is more than he knows about it, seeing that I've got more experience here than he does and he knows it?" Which may be true. And it may also be true that Darcy, Poirier, and the rest from time to time give orders on the basis of rank rather than experience; and those orders may be patently wrong and wasteful. The machine operator knows it, but the foreman won't listen.

So what. Hanrahan knows all that. He doesn't need Bruno Baron to bring him news that the back shop is awash with inefficiency, that there are men back there who would have trouble affixing a stamp to an envelope, that it is a cross between plain luck and the law of averages that keeps Quality Control's rejection rate as low as it is. He knows that what he has to work with, on all sides of him, is a solid "average." If he could unload the entire back shop and replace it with the best he could find available in the marketplace, he would be no better off. The job creates its own level of competence. When it comes to operating grinding machines, there are no superstars; there are just guys who screw up less often than others, guys who are more reliable than others, men who catch on a little quicker than others. Ironically, it is both the truly skilled and the utterly inept who are frequently the most dismal workers. Neither more nor less can be said of the front office.

The ideal worker is old Carlo Orsini, and, interestingly, it was Carlo who came away from the Hanrahan meeting with something he could use that he didn't have before.

At the moment, with his confederate, Jimmy Ouellette, beside him, he is taunting Hack Harden and the rest of the heat treat crew.

"What's the matter with you guys you don't make knives no good no more the way we did, eh, Jimmy? When we was handling the rolling mill, there wasn't nobody complaining."

"That so?" Antonio spits back. "When you old bastards was doing this work, you had five a' youse going on just the mill and you'd got another three working the heat treat. Now we got four guys, five if we gotta count the phantom over there, doing the whole thing."

"Say what you say," Carlo laughs back. "When me and Jimmy was doing it, we was doing it every day, full eight hours, not like you guys, once, maybe twice a week. Trouble with you guys is you got no experience. Youse don't know what you're doing. It's good you don't screw up more'n youse do."

"You're an old fool, you know that," yells Hack, turning his back and striding away. "Let's get outa here 'fore I forget how old and foolish these two jerk-offs are."

"Hey, Orsini," Antonio whispers as he turns to leave, "fuck you!"

"What'sa matter? You can't take a little joking? Come on, Jimmy, before Darcy comes along and makes us change their diapers."

It is understandable that old Carlo should have fallen prey to the temptation to snipe at Hack and the boys. Carlo will say that he has never been happier than since he transferred over from heat treat to the NC machines, four years ago. But he will be lying. Carlo's reputation was built at the rolling mill, not on a machine that performs to the commands of a tape printed by a secretary on the other side of the building. For forty-three years, Carlo lived in heat treat. He began work on July 22, 1935. He stood five feet seven inches and weighed one hundred and sixty-five pounds. "And I didn't have no fat on me," Carlo recalls, "just like me now." He was married and soon had three children, two of whom are currently with the company. He started at roughly thirty-five cents an hour.

By 1941, the year that Frank Pennington graduated from college and began at Pennington Inc., Carlo was making 62¢ an hour which, in 1943, jumped to 90¢. In 1956, Carlo decided he'd had enough of heat treat and bid and received a job as a drill operator. That was in the middle of November, and he had to take a cut in pay from $1.79 to $1.56 to do it. The following February, he moved on to operate the assembly machine for $1.69. In March, he was temporarily transferred back to the rolling mill at $1.93, and in April, was reassigned to the wood shop, where he made $1.75 initially and, by September, had boosted his earnings to $1.80.

But it would take a heart attack twenty-two years later to remove him from heat treat altogether. For by the end of September, 1957, he was back at "lead man" at $1.88 an hour. When he finally left, on doctor's orders, in March, 1978, he was making $5.58 an hour. Now, as an NC operator, he brings home $7.86 an hour, a little over seven dollars an hour more than he made when he started at Pennington Inc., forty-seven years ago.

For someone with as much time in one place as Carlo, his memory of his and the company's yesteryear is notably meager. He can recall the time "this guy over on K-8 was taking a crap and fell over dead." And there was the time "this guy was two-timing his old lady, so he leaves a suicide note and his hat by the oil cooling vat by the oven which no one finds until they open the next morning. So they have to drain the vat to get out the body which wasn't there anyway. Seems he grabbed a train heading north right out there on the tracks and just took off." And then there was "this guy who'd married this broad he'd met in a bar. Three weeks he knowed her and he marries her. And he thinks she's going to stay at home while he's here at work? Which she does, but only because she's a pit stop for the local cops while she's there. Then she throws the guy out and gets her cop friends to bust him once in a while for laughs. Of course he goes crazy right there in the rolling mill." And there are three suicides and some lost fingers and smashed toes and the time one of the grinding wheels broke apart and went careening over everyone's heads like a rocket and smashed against the wall by K-10.

And he can recall the founder, Arthur M., being driven around the yard in his limousine; and Frank's and Harold's father, S. R., who'd had a heart problem on top of being excessively overweight, and would come to the sliding metal door and wait until someone brought him one of the old iron-wheeled dollies, like those still in use in heat treat. Then he'd be eased onto it and someone would be assigned to yank him all over the plant. And the old man would rant and rave over lights that were on or areas that were too warm. And his opposite was Bart's father, C. W., who'd had a farm in the next township. The farm wasn't big enough to keep one hand busy year around, so winters the hand would come down and work in the woodworking shop. And when snows came, C. W. would call to the back shop and pull a bunch of the men off the machines and have them clear the driveway and the barns. He was nice the way he did it, always making sure there was coffee and maybe a little something else to keep the men warm. S. R. would call men up to his big house, too, but there wasn't ever anything extra in it for the men. With S. R. there was never anything extra. According to Carlo, if C. W. had been in charge, there would never have been any union at Pennington Inc. It was S. R. that made the back shop bring it in. "Frank's nothing like his father," Carlo says. "And Bart, he's just like his old man, only a lot smaller."

There are a few things about the past that Carlo doesn't recall, things which, if he could, might give him pause before he recommended taunting Hack Harden and the heat treat crew. For although at sixty-four Carlo has become a Pennington Inc. legend, has marked down his place in company mythology, once upon a time he was not discernibly different from the rest of the men who came in, punched in, did their jobs, and got out at quitting time. He does not recall, for instance, that when he was exactly Antonio Silva's age, his bosses graded him thus:

"Skill and ability: good; quality of work performed: normally accurate; amount of work performed: average; application to job: normal attention; cooperation with others: reasonably co-operative; absentee and tardy record: rarely."

Numerical values were assigned to each cateogry, so that the perfect employee could obtain a maximum of 260 points. The above evaluation netted him 193 points and the next one dropped him to 171. In fact, Carlo dipped as low as 151 before he pulled himself together and started back to his early high. Where Carlo lost the bulk of his points was in "application to job" and "cooperation with others," the last being his Achilles' heel.

What brought his score back up to average was "absentee and tardy." Carlo was never late. Hell could be freezing over and Carlo Orsini would be first, second, or third in line to punch in — and he would be way to the back of the line when it came time to punch out. Likewise, the list of accidents he experienced in the rolling mill reveal Carlo to be very lucky, inured to pain, exceptionally loyal, or, as Rocko Robestelli would say, "real stupid."

- 8/2/51 — Holding end of forging tongs under nazel hammer, pain in right arm at elbow: Time missed — none;
- 6/23/54 — Cutting three-and-a-half-inch steel stock on cutting wheel, wheel broke, piece stuck in mouth, breaking front tooth: time missed — none;
- 10/16/68 — forging paper knife under nazel hammer when a hot piece of scale lodged in his shoe, causing a burn on the side of his left foot: time missed — none.

The list is extensive and varied, but the result is always the same "Time missed — none." In the forty-seven years Carlo has been with Pennington Inc. he has been out twice: once in

March, 1948, for six days with a swollen elbow, the other in 1978, for five months with a heart attack.

But Carlo is becoming increasingly aware that his "iron man" stint with Pennington Inc. may be drawing to an end. This scares him. He remembers his father, who didn't live six months after being forced by the union to retire at sixty-five. For Carlo, sixty-five is less than a year away. At that time he will have forty-eight years under his belt. No one has ever come close to fifty. No one has ever reached forty-eight, but fifty, Carlo argues, is a milestone.

"What will they give me?" he wonders. "Maybe a watch," and he laughs, and worries because maybe they won't give him his chance. And maybe he doesn't want to try. Maybe it's time to relax and try something new.

So you ask Carlo: "Carlo, what do you think you'll do the first day of retirement?"

He stands there, wiping his hands on a rag that he keeps in the right rear pocket of his blue jeans. He straightens the brim of his engineer's cap. He looks around at the row of old, beaten-up green lockers, at the ancient fire extinguisher on the great iron wheels. He looks at his confederate, Jimmy Ouellette, on the other NC machine.

"I don't know," he says. "I guess I'll go down to Montana's Market Basket and get a job packing bags for three, four hours. That's a pretty good job, I hear."

15
The Shakeup

★

About three weeks ago, Antonio Silva was alone in the cutting room working on some four-foot bars, and who
should happen by but the company president, Don Schmidt.
Now, the cutting room isn't exactly on the beaten track, so
Schmidt had either become lost or had searched out Antonio
especially.

Or Schmidt was just wandering around aimlessly, looking for
someone, anyone, to unburden himself to.

Unlikely as the latter explanation may seem, it is the more
probable, for Schmidt was seen doing a great deal of wandering
at the time. He had stopped at Bruno Baron's THUNKing
bench and had asked Bruno to show him how to work a warp
out of a knife. And he'd stopped by Henry Grandmaison up in
the machine shop and asked how he liked the work.

Everybody said they thought he'd looked well. He'd seemed
very content and had even cracked a few jokes with the
men, this from a man most of them had never said a word to,
nor he one to them, although he'd always seemed friendly
enough.

But the thing that struck Antonio as strange was that Schmidt
wanted to explain why things in the company were the way
they were. It was embarrassing. It was like being cornered by
a complete stranger and being subjected to a detailed rationale
for the break-up of a marriage or, worse, a blow-by-blow description of the stranger's battle with hemorrhoids. Antonio
said he didn't take it personally and didn't understand that

much anyway, but he did wonder whether the man was Looney-Tunes.

Sean Kerouac just happened to work late, last Monday evening. The only people left in the building were the board of trustees. He was surprised because the board almost never met on Mondays. He noted that Schmidt was not there, although he had been around all day.

On Tuesday, Kerouac made a point of being in the main hall more than usual, and he noticed that Bart, Frank, and Harold were spending more time in each other's offices than usual. He also noticed that none of them stopped in at Schmidt's.

That afternoon, at the Ward 8 Club, he told his good friend Gene Scola from Production that something was going on. He could not bring himself to say what. Even after the news broke, Scola confessed that he was "shocked." "The whole thing took us by surprise," he said later to Big Gordo of the warehouse. "Come on!" Kerouac said.

A day after the Blatchford Report was issued — that is, almost two months ago — Roy Fitzgerald, the controller, wrote a note, folded it over, stuck it together with a piece of tape, nodded a bettor's nod at his assistant, Johnny Hardy, and tossed it into his desk's top drawer.

This morning, there was an announcement on the bulletin boards of the front office and the back shop. It read:

> The Board of Directors has accepted with regret the resignation of Donald Schmidt as President of Pennington Inc. Mr. Schmidt has expressed his willingness to continue to serve the company in any capacity that is asked of him.
>
> As of this date:
>> Franklin W. Pennington will continue as Chairman of the Board
>> Barton W. Pennington will serve as President
>> Harold S. Pennington will serve as Treasurer

Later that morning, Fitzgerald fetched out the note and tossed it across the desk to Johnny Hardy, who opened it, read it, and nodded a congratulatory nod. The note read: "Schmidt is a dead man."

By the time everyone had read the announcement, Harold had moved from his corner office across the hall from Hanrahan into Schmidt's front office. Schmidt had moved six years of accumulation out overnight. Hanrahan had moved into Harold's vacated office, and his office became a meeting room for Manufacturing.

Bart's first move was to come to the back shop and shake Building 1 supervisor Bud Darcy's hand. Bart and Bud go back thirty years together. They are both inveterate golfers. Bart was even wearing his blue tie with the gold number 2 irons speckled about it. As he made his way to and from Bud's office he was congratulated by the men, who smiled widely as at an old friend, and Bart returned their compliment.

His second move was to inform all department heads that he expected each to revise his budget down another fifteen percent, the very figure H. Edwin Blatchford had in mind.

The next day, Sales VP Doug Searles began sending out inquiries among his friends. A month later, he announced he was taking a job as president of a small firm in Fayetteville, New York. Bart expressed regret and then promptly took control of the department, saying that maybe he would not replace Searles, at least for quite a long time.

Within a week Bart had asked Hanrahan into his office, shut the door, and made discreet inquiries as to Hanrahan's interest in someday, perhaps even within a year or two, taking over the presidency. Hanrahan said he would think about it. He was in no hurry. First he had a union contract to negotiate. Bart wished him luck.

Leslie Gallen, Searles's secretary, got a little snookered during lunch and announced to everyone that "Schmidt was a jerk and should have been fired long ago." A twenty-two-year veteran of Pennington Inc. ways, Leslie was herself terminated three months later.

Natalie Spangler, the secretary Schmidt shared with Frank Pennington, asked for and was given the afternoon off. She was reported to be ashen-faced and speechless (which caught some attention). Schmidt would say later that of all the affiliations he made in his six years at Pennington Inc., the only person he missed was Natalie.

Natalie herself did not stay much longer. Two months later, she gave notice and left to take a "better job with better pay." This job lasted five months before she quit again, cursing that better jobs with better pay come with bigger headaches and tougher bosses than she was accustomed to. Periodically she returns to Pennington Inc. to do some private typing for Frank.

Research VP Willis Farnsworth said he was relieved. At last the company was back in family hands, he said, in hands that cared for it; not in the hands of someone who spent all his time getting rid of people who knew what they were doing, people who were irreplaceable.

Bruno Baron spent the day explaining to anyone who would listen that Schmidt had simply paid the gunfighter's price. According to Bruno, "The Penningtons don't have the heart to fire anyone, so they hired this Schmidt to get rid of people who were obviously deadweight. When Schmidt had the place cleaned up, the Penningtons simply took it back." The key was Hanrahan, Bruno said. When Schmidt hired him and the Penningtons saw how good the guy was — and seeing how Bart was free — well, from that moment on, Schmidt's days were numbered.

Hack Harden of heat treat wondered what had made Schmidt resign. "I would have thought he'd a' been around a long time," he mused to Antonio. Did the guy have another job some-where? Were things worse than Hanrahan had said they were back at that meeting?

Antonio tried to tell Hack that "resignation" meant "fired."

"They fired his ass," Antonio stated.

Hack said Antonio was full of it. The announcement said "resignation." Antonio called Hack a "dumb Canuck." Hack labeled Antonio a "frigging spic." Carlo Orsini called them both "lazy oafs," and they immediately harmonized on the question of Carlo's parentage. Then "Fuck 'Em" William Baxter suggested everyone take a break, have a cup of coffee, and "fuck 'em all anyway. Who gives a rat's ass?"

On Friday of that week, company doctor H. Edwin Blatchford told Frank and Bart that he felt the company had reached level ground and he would be reducing his time there to no more than a day a week. He said he had a waiting list of clients to minister to. There was a rental agency and a high-technology firm dealing in hospital equipment and a . . .

16

At the Crossroads

★

O n February 28, 1983, a Monday, the back shop punched out at 3:30 P.M., sharp, just as it did every weekday. The men made their ways across the yard to the parking lot beside Building 2. The afternoon was cold and overcast and still held a threat of snow, although none was predicted. Some snow did remain on the ground from Friday's surprise storm.

And just like always, they got in their cars or in with the guys they pooled with. And because it was cold they let the engines run for a while. A couple of the younger men cracked beers from six-packs they had hidden behind front seats.

As usual, Harve Grenier, the yard "lead man," stopped traffic on Washington Street and waved the men out, casting gentle obscenities at his friends as they drove past. Of course Pauly Ouellette was first out, followed by Antonio Silva. The rest followed randomly.

Only this time everybody turned right. Some kept going straight at the light, others hung a left, but ten minutes later they were all walking through the beaten, scarred door of the Franco-American Ward 8 Club, across the green on Dartmoor Street.

The Ward 8 Club is a small neighborhood social club where working men, a few women, and a bunch of local barflies come to water down and watch TV movies or hockey games. A lot of the back shop were Ward 8 Club members in good standing. Some were current or former officers. Just about all the men had at one time or another knocked down a few at the Ward 8 Club. This familiarity was one of the major reasons they had chosen to meet there in the banquet room at the rear.

The banquet room contains a pool table, a dart board, and enough card tables and folding chairs for the Friday evening rummy games that for many of the neighborhood couples is their weekend entertainment. The room also contains a pervasive, unventable odor of stale beer.

The tables were pushed into the corner. Chairs had been set in rows facing away from the bar and toward the pool table. A long serving table had been set up in front of the pool table. Union representative Charles "Curley" Michaels sat dead center, flanked by the four shop stewards, all facing the men, most of whom took chairs while a few leaned against the bar.

They were seventy-two strong, the remainder of the back shop after a long year of layoffs and shutdowns, bumpings and retirements. They weren't gathered as the back shop, however, but as fellow members of Union Local 1705 of the International Brotherhood of Allied Machinists. And their purpose was not social. They were there to vote to accept Pennington Inc.'s most recent and final contract offer — or to go out on strike.

They sat or stood in mutually sympathetic groups. Hack Harden and the heat treat crew were together off to the left; old Carlo Orsini and Jimmy and Pauly Ouellette were with Carlo's son Mickey, in the front row. The Professor stood with Hod Grady and Steve Corbett of Packing back by the bar. A few held beer bottles, most did not. All of them were somber. Some were visibly angry, but were under control. Most were confused — and a little worried. None could believe what was happening.

They were not surprised that four months of negotiations had come down to the eleventh hour. Almost all of them had been through that dance before. It was acceptable negotiating procedure. And it was no surprise that they thought the company's "final" offer was garbage. There is always some phrasing, some condition that doesn't square with the membership. They all knew that after some last-minute, under-the-gun palaver, compromises are struck, labor and management shake hands, plow under all the off-color things they've said about each other, and everyone goes back to work as though nothing much had happened. All this was par for the course, for implicit in every contract negotiation extending back forty years was the absolute certainty that the Penningtons would not let them down. You could take that to the bank.

As they waited for Curley to call the meeting to order, they tried to remind each other that that was the way it had always been. But for everyone who insisted on the point, there was another who shook his head and said: "It's different from what you're saying. You shoulda read Hanrahan's letter, you'd know better. This guy doesn't give a rat's ass for us. It's right in there." And the other would answer: "Yeah, but Bart's president." And the answer to that was: "So we got to stick it to Hanrahan." That's the way it had gone on all day, back and forth whenever, wherever the men met each other.

Hanrahan's letter. Some had it with them along with the company's proposal in the manila envelope Bud Darcy had handed to each of them as they punched out, Friday afternoon.

The "crossroad" letter, they called it, and it began:

"As an employee of Pennington Inc., you are at an important crossroad for both yourself and the company. On March 1, 1983, our existing collective bargaining agreement expires. Your decision on the offer that the company has given . . . is of particularly great importance to us — considering the general economic conditions that have affected us. . . ."

The letter concludes: "Please give this matter your greatest possible consideration."

Please give this matter your greatest possible consideration! Hanrahan's "assignment" to the back shop constituted a task of Herculean proportions, and it had to be completed in two days by a group of men whose skills lay more in the mechanics of machinery than in that of language. There were fifty-three single-spaced pages in all, the three-page letter, the proposals, five pages of supplements. The letter was in English, but the proposal was in legalese and required line-by-line comparisons with the old contract. Which was painstakingly difficult, even for the shop stewards, who had been over and over it with Hanrahan and the company lawyers during the past four months. For instance, Article 2 in the company's proposal read: "Article 2 — deleted completely; intent included under Articles 6 and 33."

What the hell was this stuff? A majority of the membership tossed the packet away after reading the first page of the letter. Some went on.

The letter was a long and somewhat labored description of the company's rationale. It touched all bases, demonstrating that for a company in clear economic peril, it was still taking remarkably good financial care of its employees. It was noted, however, that salaries as they presently stood were generous in comparison with their equivalents in the marketplace, and the company would be ill advised to offer much in the way of an increase. A supplement was included that showed the "numbers" Hanrahan had used to formulate this conclusion. But wages were not an issue. The union had recognized that point early on, and Hanrahan moved on.

"We need major improvement in productivity," he wrote. "Improvements will come with better planning, improved methods, new equipment, and more effective utilization of each of our talents and abilities."

Up to this point, those who had persevered could only debate the veracity of Hanrahan's figures and graphs which showed labor costs sweeping over falling sales with little turnabout projected. But what did the membership know? All proofs belonged to Hanrahan. Maybe the company was in bigger trouble than they thought.

As they read on, however, they began to detect storm clouds gathering. ". . . more effective utilization of each of our talents and abilities . . ." That was a tip-off. And it was closely followed by: "During the last year the difficult times and resultant layoffs have brought to my attention a distressing situation. That there is a wide range of interpretations of our labor contract and past practices."

And more: ". . . I would expect that as each of you reads through the proposal, many things may appear changed that really have not. It is only that understandings are different . . ."

And finally: "The proposal the company has submitted is how the management and owners perceive the relation [between themselves and the Union] to have been and indeed needs to be, if we are to succeed."

With "and indeed needs to be," Hanrahan had at last brought the matter to front stage, center. And if his position was still not clear to the membership all anyone had to do was check the "intent" in Article 6. There was no comparable article in the old, expiring contract. It was a brand new item, entitled: "Management Rights," and it read:

"Except as specifically limited by the express provisions of this agreement, the company retains exclusively to itself the traditional rights (as such existed prior to union organization) to manage its own business. . . ."

In other words, the company would allow the union to continue to exist, but for the first time since September 8, 1942, the company would call all the shots that meant anything. And from the members' point of view, the proposal got worse from there.

"Hitler Hanrahan," they called him. "The Sonuvabitch!" they cursed. "He's out to bust the union." "Look at what the guy's offering," they said to each other. "He knows no one's going to go for it." "Look at this," they argued. "He's trying to take away seniority. He wants to lay off anyone he wants, keep around anyone he wants. He's trying to tell us, the union, who we can bump, who we can't."

They were right. It was all in there. Those who took the time found it all spelled out. Those who hadn't taken the time took the word of whomever they customarily trusted.

By the time Curley called the meeting to order, the frustration aroused by uncertainty and disbelief warring with the tug of company loyalty had set the men up on the fence in such a straight line that no one dared predict what they would do. They all knew they hated Hanrahan and would love to tuck it to him. Most of them trusted Bart implicitly and were sure he would rescue them eventually. And even the old ones thought that maybe a lesson ought to be taught here, although they privately hoped Curley would be bringing good news from the afternoon bargaining session.

Curley gaveled them quiet. Here was the situation. As everyone knew, there had been a last-minute session and nothing had changed, except that Hanrahan had agreed to extend the old contract so that everyone could continue to work while a new contract was hammered out. There was a condition. If negotiations reached an impasse, and either side could declare it, a vote would be called. This announcement was met with a mixture of relieved sighs and wary sneers.

Now, Curley explained, there would be a vote on the compromise. If the members agreed to stay in and work while negotiating, that would be it. If they didn't, then they would have to vote on the company's proposal. If they accepted it, then that would be it; if they didn't, there was one final vote: to go out on strike.

Was all that clear? The members nodded that it was. Curley repeated the vote sequence once more. Everyone, including the older men, who seemed a little confused, said, yeah, they were ready. So, it came to the first vote — to stay in and talk, or not.

Shop steward Joe Vernon from Building 1, the oldest of the four stewards, said that much as he didn't like the company's proposal; it was better to keep working and talking than not working and just talking. He recommended the membership vote to stay in.

Vic Moffat and Dicky Schantz, Building 2's two stewards,

BUYING TIME

told the membership, "You'd be better off hanging yourselves" than staying in under Hanrahan's conditions. They both recommended a NO vote.

Pete Radack of Building 1 thought for awhile before reluctantly concluding: "I've got more than anybody to lose, but I'll go out." And while that was kind of a slip since this wasn't the strike vote, everybody knew that was what it boiled down to.

Curley himself, although only the union rep from headquarters, was close to vitriolic on the subject. He cursed Hanrahan, he cursed the company, and he said he would curse any of the membership who would even consider staying in. He promised them all that the International had "millions of dollars" in its war chest, all set aside for situations like these where management was trying to bust the union. He told them not to worry, to be strong, to stay together, and to give management a loud message.

But still there was a tide of sentiment for staying around. It seemed like the escape many of them had hoped for. The shop stewards might be three to one against but there was good sense in working and talking. It was still winter out there and . . . suddenly from the back of the room where he stood with the men up against the bar Hod Grady yelled, "Hold it!"

Hod was looking better than he had for a long time. He'd been called back for the vote from his vacation in Florida and his face was tan, his hair cut, his slacks and shirt and sweater clean and neat. Both he and Steve Corbett had lost their seats as shop stewards in the fall election, but he still commanded the respect of a number of the younger men. Hod was a rabid union man and it was well known he harbored no love for Hanrahan and imperceptibly more for the Penningtons — on general principles.

"I got only this one thing to say," Hod stated. "If we take the proposal on the old contract, we're showing a sign of weakness and they'll kill us."

The vote was thirty-nine against staying around, thirty-three in favor. There was near unanimous agreement that Hod Grady's short, impassioned speech had swayed the five votes. When Curley read the results, a quiet groan of disbelief spread around the room. A few of the old ones like Carlo Orsini and Jimmy Ouellette looked at each other and shook their heads.

There was barely any discussion on the company proposal. The defiance implied by the earlier vote guaranteed its defeat. The vote was unanimous. The vote to strike was seventy-one to one. It was said that someone had a sense of humor. No one ever owned up to it.

Gerry Hanrahan and Bart Pennington waited in Bart's office while the back shop was making its decisions. Four o'clock passed, but neither was surprised that he hadn't heard any results. It would take some time to get all the men to the Ward 8 Club and bring them to order. By five o'clock they thought they might have heard something, but still they weren't worried. They knew the back shop would undoubtedly reject the company's proposal, but they were sure — absolutely sure — that the membership would first vote to stay in and work under the old contract. Curley had proposed the compromise and had promised Hanrahan he'd sell it to the membership later in the afternoon.

Hanrahan was not enamored of the idea. He foresaw another six months of hassling with the men on the job and the negotiators at the table, and he was fed up with it. Although he would never say as much to Bart, he would as soon have the men go out. He had no loyalty to them and he knew what they thought of him. If they went out, he'd replace them, every damned one of them, and he'd made that clear to Curley and the stewards. The company was surviving, barely. The economy seemed to be leveling off and he wanted to have the back shop streamlined so that he could take advantage of any part of the upswing he could locate.

It was a hard line. It might have sounded suspiciously like a bluff. Hanrahan hoped Curley and the others wouldn't read it that way because he was prepared to make good on it. His hope was shared by Bart, who had accepted that what Hanrahan was doing was what had to be done. He didn't like it, and his acceptance was grudging. It wasn't how things had been in the past. The personal touch he had always exercised was missing from these negotiations but he knew, perhaps even better than either of his two cousins, Frank and Harold, that their company was in jeopardy and that noblesse oblige, so much the Penningtons' trademark in their personnel dealings, was out and "hard ass" was in. In other words, he was out, and Hanrahan was in.

Still, Bart was visibly relieved when Hanrahan came to him and told him about the "stick around and talk" compromise he'd agreed to. He felt now something would be worked out. Maybe things wouldn't be the same, but the same faces would be around when the changes took hold, and the "family" would go on.

Around five-thirty P.M., the phone rang. It was Curley. There had been a decision. They all agreed to meet immediately in the conference room down the hall. Curley walked in, sat down.

"Well?" Hanrahan asked.

"They voted to go out," Curley answered matter-of-factly.

There was dead silence. Hanrahan looked Curley coldly in the eye. Had he taken them out? he wondered. The guy had promised him that afternoon the membership would take the compromise. He'd virtually guaranteed it. No problem. The stewards had agreed. They'd bring in the vote. Still, he'd had his suspicions. He recalled how during a break while both sides considered the "compromise" he'd watched Curley and Vic Moffat whispering to each other, gesturing animatedly, and he'd thought, fleetingly, facetiously: "Conspirators!" He was now certain that, for whatever screwed-up reason, Curley had taken the back shop out. OK. If that was how they wanted their beds made, they could sleep in them, out beyond the chain-link fence.

"I can't believe it," Bart said after they'd locked the door behind Curley. "After all I've done for them over the years, after all my family has done, after all this company has done, they go out and do this." He went back to his office, fetched his coat, and went home, leaving thirty-one years of loyalty to the back shop "family" lying on the conference table.

Hanrahan returned to his office and called the Suffolk Police Department and ordered round-the-clock security at the gates, starting immediately. He then called the Wackenhut Corp., security specialists, and confirmed a previous call for guards at six-thirty A.M. Finally he placed a clean sheet of paper on the desk in front of him.

"Well, here goes," he said to himself. Strikes were not foreign to him. He'd driven through many picket lines during his years at General Electric. And as a boy he'd watched his father walk the lines almost annually, it seemed. So he knew strikes from both sides. However, this was the first one that he'd had something to do with causing and now had a lot to do with handling. He knew he was ready. He knew he was right. He began to write a long memo to the front office personnel.

17

Missed Signals

★

This was not the first time the back shop had struck the company. Back in 1976, they had gone out for three weeks and had come back — with a penny raise. That's the way it had always been. The men would want more money. Management would say, maybe a little more but not that much. The men would say, see you later. And after a while there would be a compromise and everybody would go back in with no hard feelings. Remember, it was all in the family.

What none of them saw this time was that, as Hanrahan had been trying to tell them for nearly a year, times had changed. All they had to do was pay a little attention to the TV news they all watched, to the newspapers they read. Why Curley hadn't spelled it out for them, no one knows, but all across the country unions were making unimaginable concessions to management, which in turn was playing its economic dirge at top volume — and then making good on its threats. Entire plants were being closed, thousands being laid off at a time. Operations were being cut to the barest of bones. It was a lousy time to go back once more to the old trump card.

But what did they know? Through layoffs and attrition the back shop had been whittled down to its oldest, most loyal, yet most insulated employees. The average tenure was now sixteen years. The majority of them lived like Pauly Ouellette. Up in the morning, off to Pennington Inc., to their respective machines, home again by four in the afternoon, lounge around, eat, watch some TV, into bed early to get up again early the next morning to repeat a cycle that almost all of them expected to keep repeating until retirement. It was a safe, secure expectation made all that much more safe and secure by their reliance on the Penningtons' "past practices and understandings."

What they also didn't know — and perhaps the fact may not have been as evident in the back shop as it was in the front office — was that Hanrahan was running the company. Frank Pennington was heading irreversibly into retirement and was spending the bulk of his time trying to keep his Marston Mixer from the ax. Bart was a reluctant president, and Harold was perfectly content being the new chief financial officer, a position that Hanrahan had suggested after having successfully orchestrated the removal of controller Roy Fitzgerald.

Ostensibly, the Penningtons controlled their own company. In reality, they sought and took Hanrahan's advice, thereby tacitly allowing a "new way of doing business" to infiltrate the front office. The increasingly nonnegotiable company proposal was Hanrahan's way of spreading his gospel over the entire company.

And the members didn't know — or at least they'd attached no significance to it — that a couple of weeks before the strike vote Hanrahan had ordered all the company's fuel tanks topped off, an obscure act that at the time caused Purchasing to frown (why top off at the end of winter, when fuel prices are at their peak and the company is supposed to be saving where it can?), but that soon became clear when picket lines formed and union drivers refused to cross over.

All the things they didn't know combined to hurt them, as they rapidly learned. The following morning, March 1, the membership gathered before the entry to the front office and the gate leading into the yard and the loading platform. It was six-thirty A.M., and cold, just starting to lighten, and everyone was geared up. The stewards had drawn up a schedule. The four three-hour watches were assigned, but that first morning they all wanted to be there when Hanrahan arrived. They had a few things to tell him about his parentage. . . .

Down Washington Street from the center of town came a large van, and it stopped at the gate. Two of the local police assigned to strike duty opened the gate. The van drew inside. The gate was pulled shut. And out of the van filed a phalanx of nightstick-wielding men in dark brown uniforms. Big, mean-looking MP types. And they took up stations before various doors and faced the membership. The Wackenhut Corp., security guards specializing in strike patrols. They were quickly renamed the "whackanuts."

"They got here awful damned fast, didn't they?" Hack Harden observed to a bunch of the strikers as they sipped coffee and glared back at the "whackanuts."

"You get the impression they was hired afore our vote?" Pauly Ouellette wondered rhetorically to his brother and Carlo Orsini and Tito Balboni.

"Fucking Hitler's out to break our balls," said Big Gordo, leaning up against the winter-leafless elm.

That same morning, Hanrahan's first memo reached the "salaried and clerical employees," that is, the front office. It began: "I have two emotions tearing into me as I write this to you — sadness and determination.

"There are many good men out on the street today, and in light of the Company position, there is no need for them to be on strike."

He then set forth an explanation of the company's positions, a sensible political move since a large number of front office employees had relatives now walking the line, and the strength of their loyalty to the company was about to be sternly tested. A number of them would be put back on machines they'd left years before.

He was quick to point out that "at the last negotiation session the Union proposed that the old contract be extended on a day-to-day basis while negotiations continued. *The Company*

156

agreed to this [the underlining is Hanrahan's]. The Union told us on leaving that they would recommend to the members that this be accepted. I don't know what happened."

Hanrahan then moved to the crux of the matter: "The Company has proposed specific articles, in as clear language as it could present, on the way in which it believes it must be able to assign work, promote, transfer, and, in general, most effectively employ the talents of its workers in order to meet the pressure of competition in the market."

And the inspiration for these articles is, he wrote: ". . . More of a need for employees to 'wear many hats' and do broader tasks . . . [and] while some of this broadening of work has taken place in the shop, it has almost always been with a hassle from someone. This is not because people are obstinate, but because there are many interpretations of the contract and associated past practices."

Obstinacy was, in reality, exactly what had galled Hanrahan ever since he had taken over Manufacturing. It was clear to him from the outset that the back shop was too fat, that there were more bodies than there was work. As he began to lop off large numbers through layoffs, the ratio of work to workers began to equalize, and before long he had reached the point at which there was more work than there were men to do it. Or so it seemed to the union. For Hanrahan this state was nearly optimum. There was no reason, he argued, to have one man per machine when with hardly any more effort that same man could operate two, even three machines. The work was not that demanding. Bull, said the union, and demanded "astronomical" pay increases for anyone forced into such labor. Each instance required extensive negotiations with the union stewards and furthered Hanrahan's resolve to be rid of this impediment to efficiency, however he could. Contract negotiations provided a ready-made opportunity.

Having thus stated his defense, Hanrahan unwrapped his offense.

"Because business conditions are still very poor, we cannot

afford to lose further revenue by a shutdown. Therefore, we have no other alternative but to begin to hire replacements . . . and to get the business back in operation."

When word of this reached the picket line, everybody laughed. No way Bart would ever let Hanrahan do it, they all said. When Hanrahan drove out through the lines that afternoon, they dared him to try it.

The next Saturday and Sunday editions of the *Suffolk Times* and the *Norfolk Record* carried the following classified ad:

DUE TO UNION STRIKE: Pennington Inc., a well-known manufacturer of machinery and industrial knives, is seeking the following personnel:

1. Machine operators skilled in setting up and operating any of the following machines:
vertical boring mills
lathes
Blanchard grinders
multispindle drills
NC drill
NC machining center
punch & shear presses
milling machines
surface grinders
knife grinders
radial drills
MC milling machine
planers
abrasive saws
2. Assemblers — mechanical, machinery and electrical
3. Tradesmen — millwrights, machinists, and tool grinders
4. Other positions — shipper/receiver/material handlers, arc welders, heliarc welders, press straighteners, wood saw operators, heat treat operators, packers, janitor tool crib/stockroom attendant, and forklift operators.
. . . These are permanent, full-time positions with good working conditions and good benefits. . . . Pennington Inc. is an equal opportunity employer.

18

The Indy 500

★

T he kid stood across the street leaning against the nearly budding oak, the slightly greening park to his back. He was dressed in worn blue jeans and a worn denim jacket, and he wore an old cowboy hat. He was young, probably in his twenties, and skinny.

He had materialized. No one had seen him get there. Anyone passing by would have assumed he was one of them. But he wasn't. They knew it. They were waiting for him, walking back and forth in front of the gate, in front of the old brick and glass building, daring him; leaning against the fence, drinking coffee, talking, grouping, then breaking up and wandering off singly or in pairs, but always watching him.

Every so often, the kid would push himself off the tree and make as if to step off the curb and into the street, then he'd sort of deflate and fall back against the tree and recommence staring at the men across the street, at the open gate and the buildings inside. And at the six local cops huddled together at the side of the street, chatting with the men.

You could see the kid was nervous, and the longer he stood there, the more nervous, the more terrified he appeared. Still, he had come that far . . . and finally he started across the street, slowly, casually, like one of them. Everyone saw him coming. The cops stopped chatting. One of them gulped the remains of his coffee and tossed the white Styrofoam cup in the gutter.

Hack Harden of heat treat left the line to meet him.

"Hack'll talk sense into him," Yogi Thomas said.

"Hey, kid," Art Moonvees yelled, and held up one of the signs that were leaning against the chainlink fence. The sign read:

"It Was Lousy On Unemployment But At Least You Wasn't A Scab"

Hack kept his hands in his pockets. He said something. The kid said something and pawed the ground with the tip of his steel-toed boot. Then Hack put his arm around the kid's shoulders and the two of them walked away up the street along the outside of the cars that were parked there. After a dozen yards the two shook hands and Hack turned around and came back, a satisfied smile on his face. The kid kept going up to the corner by the lights and disappeared over the bridge.

"What'd you tell the puke?" Harry Biondo asked.

"That the lousy company was trying to bust our union, and all us guys were giving up a lot to keep 'em from doing that, and if he crossed the line here, he'd be taking one of our jobs, and that would make him a rotten motherfucker and I'd have to break his legs. Then he says how he's been out of work for four months and he's got a wife and a new kid, but he didn't realize this was a union thing and he wished us good luck. Stuff like that."

"Fucking Hack has a way with words, don't he?"

"Yeah, but, well, I kinda feel sorry for him, but whataya going to do?"

"That's it, man. Whataya going to do?"

They were bitter. Whatever shred of loyalty remained after the arrival of the "whackanuts" disappeared entirely with the appearance of the classified ad. As far as they were concerned, the company to which they had been so loyal for so many years, the company that had taken the best they'd had to offer, had turned its back on them and was ready to treat them as though they were no more valuable than some jerk on the street. Their reaction was to dig in their heels, to shore up the line, and to declare that from then on there was the principle of loyalty involved, and that the company had been the first to break faith.

As a sign of this spirit, old Carlo Orsini, the forty-eight-year veteran, the heat treat legend, stood in line, watched the first scab cross the line, said: "Fuck 'em," and the next day went in, and quit — and continued to show up regularly on the picket line.

"Guess you'll never get that gold watch, Carlo," they laughed.

"Who'd want one of their watches, the bastards," Carlo would answer indignantly.

The irony was that Carlo had never had much use for the union and actually blamed it for killing his father by making him retire at age sixty-five.

The same day Carlo had quit, Bruno Baron drove through the lines on his way in to work in the back shop. He had his window down. He wasn't afraid of anything happening. Only two weeks before the strike vote, Bruno had been promoted to foreman. No one held it against him that he was now one of "them." They were happy. Everybody liked Bruno. So a few of the men yelled: "Scab," and Bruno gave them the finger, and the hollerer laughed as loudly as Bruno.

And when Bruno got inside Building 1, in among the now-silent, iron-cold green machines, among the stacks of knives just sitting there, when he pushed back the sliding metal door that separated the front office from the back shop and saw the lines of men — and women — filling out application forms, he knew the strike was over.

"I felt like running right out to the line and telling the men, 'Give it up. Hanrahan's serious. The place is loaded with guys and *and he's hiring.*' " He didn't. They had to know, too. These people had had to cross the lines to get in. It must all be obvious. So instead, Bruno turned on K-7 and went to work grinding an order of chipper knives. Foreman Walt Poirier had cut them. Plant supervisor Bud Darcy would be packing them in the boxes foreman John Genest was building in the wood shop. He looked around him. Half of Production was in overalls. By Jesus, they were getting work out. There was no time to worry about his friends on the line.

". . . But that night I called Wally [his stepson, a lathe operator in Building 2] and I tell him what's happening and he tells me, 'Bullshit! They'd never keep us out. Soon as we settle, the Penningtons will find a way to get rid of 'em. Hanrahan's just trying to scare us and it won't work."

"I tell him, 'Hey, you're wrong about this guy. He plays hardball. If he says they're permanent, he means it, and you guys are going to be walking for the resta your lives.' And he tells me to stuff it, which I do, and from that point on we don't talk about the strike or nothing about what I know that's going on. Of course his mother's worried and of course his wife is about to have a baby anytime. But Wally's stubborn, and if he thinks he's right on something, there's no saying otherwise."

And so the men walked the lines through the lousy, cold, damp month of March, and on the day Hack told the "cowboy" to take a hike, they'd come dressed against another day of shivering dampness. But spring dropped by for a visit, and by ten o'clock, most of them had taken off their parkas and vests and heavy sweaters and either hung them on the hurricane fence or tossed them onto the front seats of their cars.

It was like a reunion out on the line. Men who hadn't shown up for more than an hour of their assigned duty shifts came down and hung around afterward catching up on the news. The old men like Carlo Orsini, Jimmy and Pauly Ouellette, Tito Balboni, Gregory Abajian were there by the end of the first shift, went home or out for lunch, and came back for the rest of the day. It was all there was for most of them to do anyway. Coming to Pennington Inc. was what they'd been doing regularly for so many years that they didn't feel comfortable being anywhere else on a weekday.

Of course it wasn't the same as being inside and doing something. Once there, they didn't know what they were supposed to do with themselves. They stuck their hands in their pockets. They took them out again and clasped them behind their backs. They let their arms hang loose. They poked somebody on the arm or grabbed a sleeve to make a point. Some walked in an oblong circle, around and around in front of the gate. They walked singly and in pairs, chatting with each other, or silently, head down, watching the heels of the man in front. Others milled about along the hurricane fence, like steers in a feed lot. They drank coffee from the Coleman canteen set in a crate nailed to the telephone pole (Hack told them about how his wife had come down Saturday morning to walk the lines with them, had had some of that coffee and was almost instantaneously attacked by a raging case of the runs).

Big Gordo from the warehouse leaned up against the elm and stared across the fifty yards of tar to the loading dock and the two "whackanuts" standing there with walkie-talkies and notepads, jotting down things they saw. "Whataya say, Big Gordo?" someone would ask in passing, and Big Gordo would say, "Friggin' pukes!" and someone else would chime in, "You tell 'em, Big Gordo," and he'd say, "You got it."

It hadn't taken the men long to settle into a routine. The union paid them forty dollars a week, which wasn't much and for which they didn't have to do much more than show up for their appointed shifts — seven to ten A.M., ten to one P.M., one to four P.M., four to seven P.M., six days a week. Les Harper, the union secretary, checked the men off as they arrived. Les was there at seven in the morning and rarely left before six at night. There were times he wasn't sure why he was there. He didn't want to be. He wanted to be working. He had voted to stay and negotiate, but he'd gone out with the rest of them and was determined to be as long-suffering for the union as he had always been for the company. So Les kept his notes. Not only did he write down which members showed up and which didn't bother, he also counted every man who left the plant. And he took down the license plate numbers of every truck that entered the gate, and later he telephoned every company that sent a truck in, just to ask whether it was a union shop and to tell them there was a union strike in process and to ask if they would be sympathetic.

Sometimes it paid off, and a company would stop sending its truck around. Once the men thought they had the Ryder truck-rental company on their side. Pennington Inc. had rented a big yellow Ryder truck to carry cargo to shipping companies that wouldn't cross the line with their teamster drivers. Rumor had it that Ryder had agreed to honor the line and for a moment there was ecstasy on the line. But the following morning, as it had regularly since the beginning of the strike, at ten o'clock sharp, the truck rolled into sight, came around the edge of the green, the same bearded kid driving it. The cops were union men, of course. A lot of them had also grown up with some of the strikers and even now were fellow members of the Moose or Elks. So, when the Ryder truck arrived, they cleared a path very slowly, giving the men their chance to say a few things.

Which was about all the men could do. They could bitch among themselves about the heartless company, but with the exception of the epithets inspired by Hanrahan, their complaints were faint. Even those who screamed "betrayal" to newspaper reporters couldn't find it in their hearts to curse Bart Pennington, whom they had known forever. And how could they get mad at Rick Carney, the engineer, who had had to come out to the fence to ask where some bolts were stored; or at Gene Scola of Production, who comes out on Thursdays to put down a couple of dollars on the back shop's lottery; or at Guido Orsini of Quality Control, whose car was parked against the other side of the fence the men were leaning on and who made plans through the fence for supper with his father and brother.

So they yelled things like: "pukes" and "scabs," and "honey boys" at a pair of blond guys, and "superpukes" at three former union men who had been laid off and had crossed the line, and "jailbird" at a man they'd heard was up on a rape charge and was now working K-5. And they yelled things about the various ancestries of the "whackanuts." None of it sounded very friendly, nor was it meant to be, but their hearts were not in it. None of them had expected that the strike would last this long, that in fact they might really be giving up their livelihood for an abstraction like loyalty. That was not exactly how they had lived their lives so far. For another dollar more, that was a principle they could grasp. And though they had known from the outset that money was not the issue this time, most of them had imagined that this strike was going to be settled as comfortably as previous versions.

But it wasn't going to be. For those who hadn't grasped that point earlier, three weeks on the line watching more and more cars going through the gate every day were bringing the message home. Gradually it was all they were talking about. How many people had that miserable Hanrahan hired now? Someone would say: "I hear there's twenty in there." Someone else would have heard twenty-eight. There was always an optimist who had a contact in the front office, and he had heard that a couple of guys had been canned, so there were only twenty-four. And on it would go.

And when the tally wasn't the subject, lost jobs were. "Well, I heard mine's gone," one would say, and another would add that when old Carlo Orsini was in cleaning out his locker, he'd seen that both the NCs were operating and a bunch of the grinders, too, but heat treat still wasn't working. And a few eyes would turn toward Hack Harden because the betting was that Hack would be the first to break ranks and cross the line. "The louder they yell, the closer they are to cracking," the old-timers were saying, and Hack was always yelling.

The old ones were among the quietest on the line. They

knew they were through. They'd known it the minute the hiring started. No way Hanrahan wanted the old ones back. Because they knew they weren't going back, they became the cement that held the men together. They offered hope: "Maybe today they'll settle. I have a feeling it'll be today." They offered counsel: "Youse guys got to stay together. Can't anyone cross that line or the whole thing's over." They offered fuel: "You can't go back with them scabs in there as long as you got a friend that's out here and can't go back in 'cause some scab's took his job he's had for twenty years."

And everyone would nod, "That's right." They'd show Hanrahan, Bart, the rest of them what loyalty was. And they would continue walking, pacing, almost wandering. They recognized that they were in this mess together, the way they'd all been in the shop, together. But being together in the back shop hadn't made them all friends, and being on the line hadn't either. So while they walked together, they were separate, spread out the way they'd been when they were at their machines — except for the daily running of what they called the Indy 500.

How they loved their Indy 500. It was the one time each day that they could yell and scream and be utterly venomous together. It was one of the rules — and joys — of striking that there were certain times when you were expected to be animals, to be coarse, vengeful, vituperative. Even the meek, like Gregory Abajian of the boring mill, got caught up in it.

At approximately three-twenty P.M., the main doors of Building 2 would be opened and the company van would appear with the "whackanut" they called "Re-run" at the wheel. Soon you would begin to hear the "vaaroom . . . Varoom . . . VAROOM!" of the scab cars as they were brought between Buildings 1 and 2, lined up in pairs. If you stood at the corner of Washington and Beauchamp streets, you could see the first four cars. Slowly, the Suffolk police would clear a passage through the men, who would persist in walking very determinedly around and around in front of the gate, waiting until the last second to move out of the way. Then one of the security guards placed directly before the lead cars would step out of the way and with a dramatic gesture would wave the cars on.

This moment of great drama and amusement was heightened by the fact that there were a couple of cars that had seen some time up at Edgerly Race Track and were running with open exhausts.

"Here they come!" someone would yell.

Varoom-vrooming in first gear, they would edge toward the gate. Some of the men would inch up toward the path cleared by the police, making the funnel as narrow and hazardous as possible.

"Fucking scabs!"

"Super pukes!"

"Hey, sweetie, you wanta date tonight?"

The hatred the men felt toward the scabs was hearty. In the beginning the cursing had been something of a novelty. Some of the younger men had never walked a picket line before. The old-timers had never been confronted with scabs. The verbal spears they had tossed at bosses they had known for years had been good-natured. Everybody knew that strikes didn't last, were only a way of redefining territory. But this one was different, and the difference lay in the arrival of new men paid to do *their* jobs. Gradually the horror had grown on them. The scabs were the regular employees of Pennington Inc., and they, the membership, the back shop, were about to become part of the nation's alarming unemployment statistics. So when they yelled, "Super pukes" at the bodies in the passing cars, they were yelling at the faces of the enemy, and they meant it. And when they described in scatalogical detail Everett Baker of Quality Control's physical makeup, they released all tethers from their imagination because Everett Baker had brought his own son in to work. And Everett had once been one of them.

On the other side, it was a grim bunch who roared down the chute and out onto Washington Street. They knew what the story was. They knew what they had done. Many of them were sympathetic, but most of them had been without jobs for almost a year. They'd been hungry and now they were working, and those jerks on the line had given up their jobs. For what? For the opportunity to stand in the unemployment line, week after week, and tell some pale-faced beaurocrat moron that . . . yes, you had been looking for work . . . no, you hadn't found anything, maybe there was something coming, this guy was going to give you a call next Wednesday . . . then pick up the weekly check, go get the food stamps, go buy what you could, then go home again and face the old lady and the kids and the bills . . . and, worse, face that gnawing suspicion that you weren't worth the air you breathed and the proof was that no one was offering you a job.

Down the chute they'd roar, one car to the right, the next to the left, one right, one left, or six right, six left. Every day a new order to baffle and befuddle whichever picketer was assigned to follow a scab home (on the assumption that there was such an assignment), and always bringing up the end, "Re-run" in the company van following the last car until all cars were out of sight, then returning to park the car once again inside Building 2.

And across the street would stand Pat Loren, union treasurer, and Les Harper, pads of paper in their hands, doing head counts.

"Thirty-one," Les would yell out as the last car spun by him.

"I got thirty," Pat would yell back. "Anybody else got a count?"

"Thirty-one here," someone else would yell.

"I got thirty-two."

"Idiot, you counted that fucking Everett."

"That's right. Yeah, thirty-one."

On the day Hack told the "cowboy" to keep walking, everyone was in such a good mood that they laughed when the "scab count" was announced to have reached forty-four.

The next day it rained again, and those who showed up huddled together and took turns either walking the picket circle or sitting in nearby cars to keep warm. That was also the day the apple farmer Gregory Abajian learned that there was a girl doing his job on the boring machine.

"You think that's bad," Pauly Ouellette commiserated. "They got a nigger doing mine."

19

Bart's Letter

★

T here had been a moment when it had looked as though the
strike might be over. This was on March 12, a Saturday,
when the membership met at the Elks Hall. It was the first
time in two weeks they had met as a body, and there was a
growing urge to settle the strike and get back to work. The
company's proposal was not noticeably different from the one
that had been unanimously rejected. The classified ad had run
in the newspapers, however, and everyone had seen how many
men Hanrahan had hired. The arch-union men like Hod Grady
were still fanning flames, but the less committed were cooling.
They were ready for a sign from management.

They were not just ready, they were asking, almost begging
for a sign, and the proof sat in a file in the top right-hand drawer
of Bart's desk. The file was filling with letters — from families,
from friends of the families, even from some of the men themselves, each asking Bart to do something to end the strike. And
there had been telephone calls as well. The men wanted to go
back in, but they lacked what it took to cross the line and buck
what was still a majority.

Bart was torn. Most of the letters were from men, or the
families and friends of men, he had known for years, men he
had bowled with, golfed with, had shot the shit with; men he
called friends. He ached seeing them out there on the other
side of the chain-link fence, knowing how split their loyalties
were. This sympathy made his anger and frustration with leaders of the strike even more bitter than it had been after the

initial vote. He was aware that he had the power to call a halt to the whole matter, if he wanted to.

And he did, but objectively he knew that it all had to be played out across the negotiating table. He could not — he would not — undercut Hanrahan. He had made that promise to himself at the outset. Not only was Hanrahan in charge, but he was also right. The company had to come first, personal loyalties second. He accepted the argument that the ultimate demonstration of personal loyalty was a strong contract that gave the company, not the union, the right to decide what was efficient and what was not. It was the only way jobs were going to be saved, and, at that, it was not a guarantee. The company's head was barely above water and the strike was going to suck up dollars the company desperately needed to update its badly antiquated back shop. But there was no debate, an efficient crew was the top priority, and if it took a strike to effect that, that was what it would take.

Not that Bart wasn't tempted to make suggestions, especially after Frank and Harold would come in and hint that maybe something ought to be done. And maybe he would have acted if he hadn't been convinced beyond a doubt that the men knew up front what the consequences of a strike vote would be. Hanrahan had assured him that he had laid it on the line — the men could stay in and negotiate; if they went out, they would be replaced. They had voted their conscience. Bart was satisfied.

And lest there be any misunderstanding of his position, Bart sat down and composed a letter, which was distributed to each of the men as they gathered for the March 12 vote. The letter was strictly Bart's, although it was approved by Hanrahan. It read:

"I would like to clear the air," he wrote, ". . . of [the] many half truths . . . being circulated regarding this strike."

"First and foremost," he continued, "the Company is not trying to break the Union. Our proposal . . . clearly recognizes the Union. . . ."

From there Bart went on to emphasize that contract negotiations had traditionally been the responsibility of the vice-president of Manufacturing. He then reiterated the need for language clarification, noting that "even before Gerry Hanrahan
came to Pennington Inc." there was a need for a "better understanding of the interpretation of language, some of which went
back as far as 1942," and nearly all of which he had been party
to, he could have added.

Having placed his signature to the rationale behind the company's proposal, Bart followed with a full-fledged endorsement
of his Manufacturing VP: "I am in full accord with everything
offered or proposed by Gerry Hanrahan."

In conclusion, he stated that "Pennington Inc. is a family-
oriented business. We are not for sale" (which was one of the
rampant, "for sure" rumors on the line). "We are also a family-
oriented business throughout. Today we have divided families
—sons on the strike picket lines and fathers, brothers, and re-
lations at work in supervision. All have earned a living here
over many years.

"Pennington Inc. has been a good place to work. It will continue to be a good place to work under the proposal the Company has made and which will be voted on today."

Reaction to Bart's letter on the part of the members of Local
1705 of the international Brotherhood of Allied Machinists il-
lustrated how completely severed the lines of "past understandings" had become. It is nearly impossible to discern from
that letter any position other than a four-square endorsement
of Gerry Hanrahan. Yet, there were many members of the
union so convinced that Bart would step in and rescue them
from Hanrahan's tyranny that they saw in this letter the long-
awaited sign that Bart was about to make his move. Ironically,
it was shop steward Vic Moffat, the most vocal representative
on the negotiating team, who stood up before the vote, shook
the letter, and told the members not to accept the company
proposal because Bart was on the way.

There were others, like Hod Grady, who laughed and said

the letter demonstrated conclusively that Bart and all the rest had sold out. Bart was never going to come.

Both sides were guessing, but the vote was unanimous. The company proposal was rejected again. Monday the members were back on the line. There was general agreement that Bart's letter had been a deciding factor.

And on Monday, Hanrahan wrote another of his memos to the front office. If the union were looking for a signal, Hanrahan's memo was it.

First, he informed everyone that "a higher level of security" had been established, both inside and outside the plant. He said he had the assurance of the Suffolk police chief that "his men would do their job."

There had been some question as to whether the six patrolmen assigned to the gates were enthusiastic protectors of the company's property and whether the chief was truly paying attention. It so happened that the chief was actively running for mayor and saw more votes on the line than inside the front office. Also, many of the patrolmen were fellow Elks, former classmates, or both. They were also union men.

Hanrahan then issued a rallying cry to the front office that rang with echoes of the long-since-departed former president, Don Schmidt.

"Out of this adversity we will rebuild a shop operation and a business that will meet and then beat any of the competition in the marketplace. . . . These difficulties have brought us closer together, and just as families draw together to support each other in hard times, so can we in our work. . . . Don't hesitate to ask for help with problems. It will be given."

Some of the older fixtures in the front office insisted that Bart Pennington was still in charge, that Hanrahan was no more than a hatchet man for Bart, that Hanrahan would go the way of Schmidt when he had the back shop all neatened up. The newer personnel understood the significance of Hanrahan's tag line:

"As I see the beauty of the morning sun unfold after so long a period of rain, I cannot help but think it is auspicious and that through what lies ahead there will be many good times and fine associations for all of us."

The old ones said that Hanrahan was getting a swelled head, and that Bart would take care of that problem later.

At the bargaining session two days later, Hanrahan introduced the "open shop" condition. In its final form it reads:

"Employees outside the bargaining unit (Union) shall be permitted to perform the work of any employee in the bargaining unit so long as it does not directly result in the layoff of a Union employee in the foreseeable future. . . . Nothing in this article shall be construed as requiring employees to join or refrain from joining a labor organization. . . ." In other words, you no longer had to be a union member to work at Pennington Inc.

The "open shop" article became as immutable as the seniority, layoff, bumping, transfer, and rehiring articles the company had stood by firmly from the beginning. At the point when the "open shop" article made its appearance on the negotiating table, Local 1705 ceased to be an effective bargaining unit. It was only a matter of time before the separate pieces that made up the unit would begin to spin off.

20

The Breaking Point

★

S trike headquarters is across the green in an old blue wood-framed apartment house. The tenants are single, middle-aged men and women, most of whom hold some sort of job. Their apartments are the most recent in a lifelong series of moves around the city. So, generally, are their jobs.

The "headquarters" is the Professor's apartment. It is on the first floor, rear, second door to the right. It consists of one high-ceilinged room and a bathroom tucked out of sight around to the left. The refrigerator is on the left as you enter, the stove and sink to the right against the hall wall. There is a plugged fireplace and a mantel along the right wall, then a series of three windows that wrap around the head of the Professor's bed to the solid left wall, which returns to the bathroom door.

The refrigerator contains a gallon of milk, some beer, bread, and mustard. Beside it is a table piled high with cartons, Styrofoam cups, and miscellany. Under it is a large cardboard box filled with dog-eared paperbacks. On the counter beside the sink is a twenty-four-cup coffeepot, hot with refill for the Coleman jug that stays on the line. There are dishes and pans, dirty and clean, in and near the sink.

There is a card table in front of the fireplace, a chair in front of it, some papers and envelopes, and a red telephone on top. On the mantelpiece are stacks of books, paper cups, more miscellany, and two wide-mouth jars, one filled with pennies, the other with larger change. The latter is picket-line coffee contribution. The former is the Professor's. There is also a black-and-white framed photograph. It shows two pre-teenage children and their father and mother sitting on the stairs of a porch: the Professor, his late wife, and their children. The kids are now grown and have their own families. There are no pictures of them. The wife has been dead, of emphysema, for ten years. In the picture she is holding a cigarette. The Professor seems very content. Those were apparently very good days.

Next is a television set. *The High and the Mighty* is the afternoon rerun. Nearby from a radio a talk show is gabbing. There is a bureau beside the television and, leaning up against the bureau, is a pile of picket signs. Some of them read:

— Hanrahan Doesn't Want Good Men. He Wants Scabs He Can Pick When They Fester —

— You Are Not Taking My Job — You Are Giving Up Your Dignity For Hanrahan's Lie —

— If the Benefits Were As Good As They Say They Are, I Wouldn't Be Here — BEWARE —
23 Years On The Job And They Shit On Me. What Do You Think They Will Do To You —

— Hanrahan — May The Bird Of Paradise Shit On Your Head —

— Reagan Has Screwed Up The Country — Hanrahan Has Screwed Up Pennington Inc. — Now That's A Pair That Russia Can Have — Please —

On the right hand side of the bed is a small table with a makeshift CB receiver taped down on the top, this is used to monitor police calls or conversations between incoming or departing truckers and their dispatchers. On the left-hand side of the bed along the wall are two easy chairs. The bed is a mattress on a box spring, with a brown blanket pulled over it like a spread.

The Professor sits on the edge, facing the open window, reading a Ross MacDonald mystery. Once in a while he looks out the windows and laughs.

"The crazy jerk in Apartment Two. First he throws feed out for the wrens, then the blue jays come, so he heaves rocks to scare them off and scares off the wrens with them. That guy deals from a short deck."

Union treasurer Pat Loren sleeps spread out in one of the easy chairs. His thick-lipped mouth hangs slack.

Shop steward Vic Moffat paces back and forth from the end of the bed to the door. Once in a while he opens the door and yells, "Hey, Molly, got some spaghetti sauce for me to eat?" then breaks into a cackle. "Guess Molly ain't home today. I could use a little of her sauce right about now." Then he whirls his CAT cap around with his index finger and begins to pace again. "What a scuzz bag!"

Shop steward Dicky Schantz sits by the phone, doodling on a yellow legal pad. "That fucking Tito Balboni's been walking the line all morning complaining how there's no more Blue Cross and what if he has a heart attack," Dicky suddenly erupts. "That's just what we need, some guy getting everybody all stirred up about something he don't know shit about. How many times you got to tell some of these guys they got another month covered, that they don't get canceled without notice? Jerks!"

Hod Grady sits on the foot of the Professor's bed, cleaning his fingernails. His face is still tan from the interrupted Florida vacation that now seems so long ago. Hod still thinks of himself as one of the stewards although six months ago, he was replaced by Joe Vernon, who is sitting next to the sleeping Pat Loren, eyes riveted on the TV.

"When's the next negotiation session?" Hod asks.

"You'd come down to the line more often, you might find out," Joe Vernon answers, his eyes not wavering from the black and white screen.

"Up your ass! . . . How long Sleeping Beauty here's gonna lie there? I need some bread. . . . Hey, Sleeping Beauty, I need my check. . . . Jesus, look at'm. What a lazy bastard!"

Suddenly something flies through the air and lands with a thud on the floor near the bathroom door. It is the Ross MacDonald mystery.

"Well, that's another dead one." The Professor stretches and stands up. "Guess I'll walk over and see what's going on over on the line. Anyone coming?"

The three union leaders just stare at him.

"Dumb question," the Professor admits and, wriggling himself into a fraying Pennington Golf Team jacket, walks out the door.

Gerry Hanrahan sits at a round table for two in the lounge of the Towne Lyne Restaurant, a St. Pauli Girl and a plate now only half-full of lukewarm toasted cheese Nachos in front of him. Outside, it is dark; inside dimly lit, and the lights of the passing cars flash like signals on the plate glass window beside him.

The beer is his third, the hors d'oeuvres his first. He is on his way home to a later supper. The Towne Lyne Restaurant is just enough out of the way that the chances of running into anyone from work are negligible. He wants to relax.

He is wearing a brown tweed sport coat, a white shirt, the collar open and the knot of the brown tie pulled down past the second button. He is leaning back without tipping his chair, and his legs are crossed. The sport coat hangs slightly open to his side and the handle of a revolver shows from the holster strapped under his arm.

"You know, a funny thing happened as I was leaving the plant today," he is saying. "As I drove out the gate, I heard one of them yell out, 'Hanrahan, you're a fucking Communist bastard!' and all I could think of was: God knows with six kids they got it part right. But a Communist? No, fella, you're wrong there. One hundred and eighty degrees wrong."

And he laughs, then leans forward, elbows on the table. He stares out the window for a while before continuing.

"The whole thing's stupid, you know. Another couple of weeks and I'll have 'em all replaced, all because these guys won't accept change. It was their choice. They made it. I didn't have a choice. If we didn't change, it would be a matter of time before we'd all be on the street. That's a fact.

"You see the irony? These guys are on the street now and the only way they're going to survive is if they change."

Hack Harden of heat treat crossed the line at seven o'clock, Monday morning, April 4, he and Bill Borden of Shipping. They walked up to Les Harper, the union secretary, and handed him their formal resignations from the union. Les refused to accept them, so they stuffed them into his hand, turned around, crossed the line, and went back to their old jobs.

It was about the worst thing that could have happened to the membership, for it brought out into the open the fear that was beginning to grow in all of them. It was one thing when old Jimmy Ouellette's son Gary went down the road and got a better job. That was not a defection, and everyone was happy for him. And it was well known that a lot of the men had applications in for jobs all over the city, and that they were saying, "If I ever get this, I'm gone. I'll never work at this low-rent place again."

And at least half the men had found part-time work in warehouses or laying carpet or cleaning up yards. They weren't bringing much in, but no one was able to live off the forty dollars the union was doling out. If anyone knew anyone who might have work or might know where there was some, phone calls were made. Those who had wives working were in better shape than those who didn't, but few had money in the bank and a month times forty dollars a week was stretching them all to the breaking point.

But no one had crossed the line. It is hard to say why they hadn't. Most of them were simply scared of what the others

might say or do. And the longer they stayed out, the more detailed became the description of violence that would be
wreaked. Yet most of them were privately thinking that the
whole strike was stupid, had always been stupid, that they had
been stupid and were still being stupid, and they should smar-
ten up and start thinking about themselves, about their families, about Number One.

That's how Hack Harden finally reconciled it. "I said to myself, it's time to take care of the big one. I could see we weren't
going to win this thing. Anybody could see that. You could see
what was happening. We were giving up our jobs to guys that
didn't have jobs because there weren't any out there to have.
Hanrahan had us by the balls and he wasn't going to let go."

And Hack was right. Management owned the cards and was
doing the dealing, and the union had to take what was given.
Which at that point was a chance to work — on management's
conditions. With each succeeding day, there were fewer
chances, which added up to more men on the street. And the
more men there were who knew they could not go back in because their jobs were taken, the greater became the pressure
to stick together, to tough it out, to go down as a body, a little
like Custer's troops.

So the men yelled and called Hack and Bill "everything but
white." And that was all. They said they would do a lot of things
that would have made even a "lifer" tremble, but saying was
the extent of it. The damage had been done. Deflation set in.
Over in strike headquarters the leadership sat drinking coffee
and passing around a letter that had appeared in the Letters
section of the *Suffolk Times*. "This is saying it the way it is,"
they assured each other in a buoying tone. The letter read:

> I am writing this concerning the Pennington Inc. strike. It is
> amazing that in this day and age a company can get away with
> such unjust treatment of the working man.
>   Where would Pennington Inc. be if it wasn't for these hard-
> working, loyal employees. These men had no choice but to

strike; if they didn't, they would have taken a step backwards.

Some of these men have worked there for over forty-five years and this is what they get in return. Most of these men have families to support, and with today's economy that isn't easy with or without a strike.

If this country was made up of men like these we would be in a lot worst condition than we already are.

Where is the justice in all this — what do they hope to gain? I know a lot of people feel the way I do and I hope more people will understand the plight of these strikers. I give them all the credit they deserve.

"Who wrote that?" the Professor asked, having walked into the room late.

"Somebody named Willa Rodgers," Hod Grady said. "I never heard of her but she writes pretty good."

"Shit," said the Professor, "Willa Rodgers! That's the broad Jimmy Ouellette's kid Gary lives with."

"Who gives a rat's ass! She still writes good," Hod snapped.

"Who gives a rat's ass is right," said the Professor, who then stretched out on his bed and began reading.

21

The Final Settlement

★

The Friday afternoon vote at the Ward 8 Club had little to do with the company's contract proposal. The strike was a month and a half old. Negotiations were on the verge of impasse. Savings accounts had dried up, and the latest "scab count" was fifty-two. The only issue remaining to the members of Local 1705 of the International Brotherhood of Allied Machinists was whether the majority would allow the minority to go back to the remaining jobs or whether it would let its now torpid bitterness take everyone down.

There was actually never much doubt as to the outcome. That morning the men gathered and walked the lines perfunctorily. They knew it was the last time they'd have to be there. They knew it was the last time most of them would see each other again. The younger men talked about prospects, about brothers-in-law who knew somebody over in Altoona who was hiring, they thought. Art Matchek, who'd been on grinders for ten years, guessed maybe he and his father would go ahead and buy that secondhand Diamond Reo cab they'd been looking at and try some short-distance hauling. Steward Dicky Schantz, who had been moonlighting laying carpet, said it wasn't a bad line of work and maybe he wouldn't go back in even if the company said he could come.

Old Jimmy Ouellette talked about selling his house in Suffolk and moving out to Arizona, buying a trailer, and settling into a park next to his sister. Carlo Orsini said he didn't know what he was going to do. Maybe he'd mow the lawn when the grass began to grow, which couldn't be too far off. Pauly Ouellette said he had work to do on his house and anyway the Mrs. still had her job and maybe there would be something over to Tabor Industries, where she worked.

But most of the older men just paced back and forth and talked about the old days, about some of the machines in the plant they'd worked, about some of the foremen, the good ones, the bad ones. And then they'd stop talking and just keep on walking, back and forth, turning at invisible points and starting back as though they had spent their lifetimes in a cell just so long, just so wide. These weren't the men who were old enough to take early retirement. These were the fifty-five-, and fifty-seven-year-olds who had long ago settled into their niches and had planned to stay ensconced until the Final Friday came. They had always suspected that they had outlived their "market value," but that hadn't bothered them because they knew they had value to Pennington Inc. They knew they could do their jobs as well as anyone around and that as long as they obeyed the written and, more important, the unwritten "past practices" rules, they would be safe from the world's harm. And now they were about to be cast adrift.

They all knew this about each other as they walked the line that Friday morning, and for some reason they were still in a good mood. In fact, they had come to laugh. It was so crazy. They would have agreed with Hanrahan. There had never been any reason for the strike. They laughed when the Suffolk police told them in the morning that this was their last day, too. The company had already informed the station that as of five-thirty P.M., it would have no more need of their presence (five o'clock would be one hour after the vote should have been taken). They laughed when one of the "whackanuts" came to the fence and said, "I'm glad you're going to settle this thing so's I can get back to collecting myself."

And they laughed that afternoon for the last time at the Indy 500. And for the first time, no one bothered to take a "scab count."

The following Monday morning Hanrahan came in earlier than usual and sat down to compose his last strike memo to the front office: "The Union membership met late Friday afternoon and voted to accept the Company's last proposal. This vote brings the strike to an end. . . ."

He spent most of the day in his office, consulting with his foremen and superintendent Bud Darcy. He did not go into the back shop. The strike was over; the hard work was now at hand. He had won the contract he'd said he needed. He had just the amount of manpower he figured was necessary. He'd gotten rid of the "hard cases" (better yet, they had gotten rid of themselves). There were new rules, new regulations, no old understandings. For the first time since he had taken over almost a year and a half earlier, he was unilaterally in charge of manufacturing.

The price he'd had to pay was heavy. The strike itself had cost the company a quarter of a million dollars in security payments and lost revenue. And it might be worse. There were old customers to be won back, new customers to be convinced. A lot of expertise had been lost, and it was going to take time to train the new men, a lot longer than Darcy and the foremen would admit. Hanrahan was under no illusions concerning the quality of the new help.

All day long he wished he could be excited.

The *Suffolk Times* headlined the story: "Pennington Strike Settled; 20 Are Rehired."

Among the twenty union members rehired was Joe Vernon, the steward who recommended that the men continue working while negotiating. Joe returned to his old job on K-12. He looked around and saw two kids he thought he recognized from the Indy 500. He went over and introduced himself, then flicked the switch, looked at the yellow operation sheet in front of him, and began setting the angle of the grinding wheel.

The two most vocal stewards, Vic Moffat and Dicky Schantz,

were not rehired. In the newspaper account, Hanrahan said that "their positions as negotiators had nothing to do with the decision not to hire the two men."

The fourth steward, Pete Radack, who had reluctantly advised the members to go out, was taken back. He refused for a couple of days on the grounds that Hitler was an apt nickname for Hanrahan and he wanted no part of the sweat shop he expected Building 1 would become. He came back on Wednesday. The first thing he noticed was a sheet on the bulletin board beside the time clock:

(1) DO NOT PLAY RADIOS, TAPE RECORDERS
(2) DO NOT READ MAGAZINES, NEWSPAPERS
(3) COFFEE BREAKS: BUILDING 1 — 8:45–8:55; 2:45–2:55

The Professor returned and took up his seat in the corner of the packing room. To his surprise the Len Deighton paperback he'd stuffed into the drawer as he was leaving for the strike vote over a month earlier was still there. That was all he needed to feel at home. After a couple of hours he'd forgotten that Hod and Steve weren't there anymore.

Antonio Silva came back to heat treat, but his return was clouded. On the previous Friday, he had walked the line, gone to the Ward 8 Club, voted to accept the company's proposal, had stayed around afterward and had a few drinks with some of the membership, contributed his fair share of defamation of Hanrahan, never letting on that two days earlier, he had contacted plant supervisor Bud Darcy about having his old job back if he quit the union. Bud had given thumbs up, but Antonio might have kept the faith and stayed in the union had he not overheard union treasurer Pat Loren saying he was going to make sure Harve Grenier got the remaining heat treat slot. Antonio left the club, went home, called Darcy for confirmation, received it, and on Saturday, resigned from the union. And none too soon. On Sunday night, Harve Grenier made a call to Darcy, who told him the slot was already filled.

Foreman, former THUNKer Bruno Baron reportedly came near tears that Monday morning when the remaining twenty arrived for work. A lot had changed for Bruno since he had been moved to the "other side." It hadn't taken him long to "see things from another point of view," to realize that the facts upon which he had built so many of his familiar theories had hitherto unsuspected shadings. So while he had sympathized with his former union brothers, he knew they had been wrong, that they were suffering from delusions. He had wanted to tell them that things had changed forever, but it was all right. Maybe things wouldn't be the same, but maybe they'd even be better.

And like the rest of the foremen, like superintendent Darcy and Production's Scola, even like Bart himself, Bruno wanted to extoll the virtues of the new men in the back shop. He would say things like: "It's unbelievable how much better these guys work" and "These guys have so much talent, so much drive, already so much loyalty and dedication to the company. It's . . . fantastic!"

And Bruno believed it! Still, when Hack Harden crossed the line, Bruno was the first to shake his hand and welcome him back to the "family." And when the twenty punched in and walked as naturally as ever to their respective machines, Bruno had to hold back tears. At last everything was back to normal.

Company president Bart Pennington stood at the window of his office, a cold cigar in the corner of his mouth, his hands in his pockets. He was in shirtsleeves. A Midway Transport truck was backing up to the loading dock. A forklift was scooting around the corner of Building 1. He couldn't tell who was driving it. From where he was standing, there was not a single sign that anything out of the ordinary had taken place. Everything seemed to be the way it always had been.

There was a knock on the door, which then opened slightly and Gladys Hale, the receptionist, stuck her head in.

"Coffee, Bart?" she asked.

"Please," he said, mechanically.

Epilogue

On March 2, 1984, a year to the day the back shop set up its
picket lines, two years and a week after H. Edwin Blatchford
issued his "shape it up" report, Gladys Hale sits in her receptionist's cubicle behind the sliding glass window at the rear of
the front lobby and answers an in-coming call: "Pennington
Inc. May I help you?"

As it has every time for thirty-three years, her tone seems to
ask: "Wh'd' you want?" Hell has come close to freezing over
twice in the past two years, and Gladys hasn't changed a bit.

Nor, it seems, has Pennington Inc. There are fewer cars in
the front office and back shop parking lots, but the cars there
are the same, parked in the same places. The furniture in the
lobby hasn't been rearranged. The plaques on the wall haven't
been updated, the most recent still being a civic award — 1965.
The halls remain a milky green.

The Honor Roll across from the bulletin board by the ladies'
room is current, which seems to imply that Ida Bright is still
around. She is, although her office has been moved to make
room for Gerry Hanrahan, who has taken over the personnel
director's office. This places Hanrahan in line with executive
row, which begins with president and acting Sales VP Bart Pennington, chief financial officer and Administration VP Harold
Pennington, and chairman of the board Frank Pennington,
who has yet to retire, as rumored.

There are no new faces in the front office, just fewer faces, a
year older. John Hardy is there, still slurping through his pipe,

pushing Amway products when not acting as controller. Gene Scola is in his cluttered office, a little heavier, a bit balder, even more intense now he is in charge of all purchasing for Building 1. And his friend from the Ward 8 Club, Sean Kerouac, sits before a System 34 terminal, still working to bring MAPICS on line, his position with the company growing more secure the closer he gets.

Some faces are missing, but the "old faces" have to be reminded who they belonged to: Don Schmidt? — "Don't know whatever happened to him. Wasn't he starting up some consulting business?"; Doug Searles? — "Haven't the slightest idea. Didn't he go out of state?"; Roy Fitzgerald? — "Let's see . . . that guy . . . Don't know"; Tommy Lee McRainey? "Who? Oh, yah, him. Who knows?"; Dan Hutton? ". . . ?"

Willis Farnsworth is still there, but the arena in which he is accustomed to holding forth has been dramatically scaled down. Willis no longer commands full control of the Pennington Research Center. There is still room on the floor for part of a demonstration Whirlwind, but the machine is nearly buried behind giant rolls of paper and boxes. A huge, hunter green Marston Mixer now dominates the room.

This is not a sign the Whirlwinds are out and Marston Mixers are in. It does signify a major change in direction, however. The Mixers, Whirlwinds, and Flomacs, all capital goods that Frank Pennington has worked so diligently over the past two decades to excite the marketplace about are out. All of them are now sold on an accidental basis. If a company is interested and willing to pursue the matter on its own initiative, Pennington Inc. will oblige. However, Pennington salesmen do not carry brochures in their briefcases. (Willis continues to badger Sales to "get on the stick," but his credibility has suffered over the past two years. A number of Whirlwinds have literally shaken themselves apart, the result of overselling and underdesigning on Willis's part. The cost to the company for repairs has canceled out what profit might have accrued.)

The Marston Mixer in PRC represents at once sad defeat and sweet victory for Frank. While it is the end of the line for the Mixers, which Frank remains convinced would eventually come into their own and provide substantial profit, this one stands as the means by which the company might still make some additional monies. The Japanese deal Doug Searles dedicated his last company energies toward has come through. Frank and the Japanese have provided convincing figures for "company doctor" H. Edwin Blatchford. The joint enterprise has been in operation for almost a year and is expected to be turning a profit soon.

Like the front office, the back shop appears unaltered by the crises of the past two years. To anyone only casually familiar with Building 1 everything seems to be in order. The same smells are there, the same oily patina over everything, the same sooty windows, the same great green machines, the same yellow lines, the same iron-wheel carts, the same battered pallets with stacks of knives. The same faces. Almost.

After the strike there had been mostly new faces along with new routines and new practices and understandings. The new Beginning. That was a year ago. Since then there has been some settling. Attrition has taken place. A lot of new faces have given way to old faces. The union–nonunion split is now nearly fifty-fifty. The "family" has begun to regroup. And new ways have begun to resemble old routines, perhaps just because there are only so many ways of doing the same thing.

Hack Harden and Antonio Silva are still there and neither has chosen to rejoin the union, which they'd left to get their old jobs in heat treat back. The Professor is in Packing, Big Gordo is now the company gofer, all six feet three inches of him stuffed into the seat of the Pennington van which five-foot-four-inch Pauly Ouellette had bounced around in for so many years.

Pauly is not there. He is home, making models in his basement and having breakfast every Thursday morning with old

EPILOGUE

Carlo Orsini. Carlo and his longtime friend from heat treat and NC machine days, Jimmy Ouellette, were brought into the front office after everyone had cooled down from the strike. At the conference table they were presented with certificates of honor for their long and faithful service to the company. Bart presented them. Frank came and shook hands. The two men did not receive the traditional "cash bonus" because no hat had been passed on their behalf. Hardly anyone in the back shop knew these two men, who between them had amassed ninety-four years at Pennington Inc. Carlo also did not get the gold watch he guessed the company would probably give him. He did get a job packing bags at Montana's Market Basket, as he guessed he would. Old Jimmy sold his house and moved to a trailer park in Arizona, where he joined his daughter and two sisters.

Most of the old faces have disappeared from memory: Gregory Abajian, the apple farmer? Tito Balboni of the lottery chances? Henry Grandmaison, the dreaming machinist? "Fuck 'Em" William Baxter?

The rolling mill has also disappeared. The twin forges, the great flywheel and the rolling machine, the hammers, everything in that dark, far corner of heat treat is gone. In their place is a very broad, very deep hole, squared off with poured concrete walls and footings. A large sheet of clear polyethelene hangs from the girders and walls the area off from the rest of Building 1.

Plant superintendent Bud Darcy stands at the edge of the hole and with sweeps of his hand one way, sweeps another, he explains how the knives of Pennington Inc.'s future will run along an overhead track and will be lowered by the pressing of a button into the new brazing furnace, which in a few weeks will fill the hole. The new knives will be harder, more durable, more reliable. They will be on the revolutionary edge of the market and will put Pennington Inc. into the vanguard, a place it hasn't occupied since . . . since . . .

Darcy cannot remember when the company was ever in the vanguard of any market. Perhaps when the grandfather, Arthur W., started the company in 1905? Maybe when the father, S. E., introduced the very forges now being replaced? In the thirty years he has been with the company, it has always run with the pack. But no longer. Darcy is ecstatic.

"This is our future. Right here," Darcy states confidently, pointing into the hole.

DATE DUE

GAYLORD 234			PRINTED IN U. S. A.